D0467571

The Hell with Love

The Hell with Love

POEMS TO MEND A BROKEN HEART

EDITED BY
MARY D. ESSELMAN
AND ELIZABETH ASH VÉLEZ

WARNER BOOKS

NEW YORK   BOSTON

"Quick and Bitter" by Yehuda Amichai, from *Poems of Jerusalem* and
Love Poems: A Bilingual Edition. Copyright © 1992. Reprinted by per-
mission of Sheep Meadow Press.

"Cigarettes" by John Ash, from *The Burnt Pages.* Copyright © 1991 by
John Ash. Reprinted by permission of Carcanet Press, Ltd.

Copyright information continued on page 232.

Warner Books

Time Warner Book Group
1271 Avenue of the Americas, New York, NY 10020
Visit our Web site at www.twbookmark.com.

Printed in the United States of America

First Printing: January 2002
10 9 8 7 6

Library of Congress Cataloging-in-Publication Data
   The hell with love : poems to mend a broken heart / edited by
   Mary Esselman and Elizabeth Vélez.
       p. cm.
     ISBN 0-446-67854-6
     1. Love—Poetry. 2. Separation (Psychology)—Poetry.
     3. Loss (Psychology)—Poetry.
   I. Esselman, Mary. II. Vélez, Elizabeth.

   PN6110.L6 H45 2002
   808.81 '93543—dc21   2001026259

Book design and text composition by Ellen Gleeson
Cover design by Janet Perr

Dedicated to our students and our teachers—
you know who you are

Contents

Introduction   *xiii*

Rage   *I*
WHEN HATRED ISN'T STRONG ENOUGH

MARGARET ATWOOD	"you fit into me"	*9*
MICHAEL FRIED	"Somewhere A Seed"	*10*
GWENDOLYN BENNETT	"Hatred"	*11*
JOHN DONNE	"The Message"	*12*
LOUISE GLÜCK	"Unwritten Law"	*14*
YEHUDA AMICHAI	"Quick and Bitter"	*16*
LOUISE GLÜCK	"Mock Orange"	*18*
LUCILLE CLIFTON	"wishes for sons"	*20*

Sadness   *23*
WHEN YOU'D RATHER DIE THAN EAT OR SLEEP

LOUISE BOGAN	"Solitary Observation Brought Back from a Sojourn in Hell"	*33*
EMILY DICKINSON	"After Great Pain"	*34*
BILLY COLLINS	"Some Days"	*35*

CONTENTS

WILLIAM CARLOS WILLIAMS	"The Widow's Lament in Springtime"	37
JOSEPH STROUD	"The Song of Divorce"	39
LARRY VÉLEZ	"Chinese Dragons"	40
JAMES WRIGHT	"Lying in a Hammock at William Duffy's Farm in Pine Island, Minnesota"	42
MARILYN HACKER	From "Coda"	43
JOHN ASH	"Cigarettes"	44
WILLIAM SHAKESPEARE	excerpts from *Hamlet* and *Macbeth*	47 48

Self~Hatred 49
WHEN YOU'RE CONVINCED IT'S ALL YOUR FAULT

LOUISE BOGAN	"Women"	59
GWENDOLYN BROOKS	"my dreams, my works, must wait till after hell"	61
SANDRA CISNEROS	"The Heart Rounds Up the Usual Suspects"	62
STEVE KOWIT	"Cosmetics Do No Good"	64
MARGE PIERCY	"A Work of Artifice"	66
SHARON OLDS	"I Go Back to May 1937"	68
PHILIP LARKIN	"This Be the Verse"	70
JOSEPH STROUD	"Memories at the Movies"	71

False Hope 73
WHEN YOU'RE CONVINCED YOU CAN GET BACK TOGETHER

PABLO NERUDA — "If You Forget Me" — 82
GALWAY KINNELL — "The Vow" — 85
MICHAEL DRAYTON — "Since There's No Help" — 86
COVENTRY PATMORE — "A Farewell" — 87
ELIZABETH ASH VÉLEZ — "Elvis P. and Emma B." — 89
JUANA INÉS DE LA CRUZ — "I Can't Hold You and I Can't Leave You" — 91
CAROLYN CREEDON — "litany" — 92

Resolve 97
WHEN YOU'RE DETERMINED TO MOVE ON

DOROTHY PARKER — "Résumé" — 105
ALICE MEYNELL — "Renouncement" — 106
MARIE PONSOT — "One Is One" — 107
DEREK WALCOTT — "Winding Up" — 108
EDGAR BOWERS — "Amor Vincit Omnia" — 110
ELIZABETH BISHOP — "One Art" — 111
LOUISE GLÜCK — "Lute Song" — 113

Relapse

WHEN YOU'D GIVE ANYTHING TO GO BACK

TOM SIMON, ED.	"Sunshine"	*126*
ROBERT FROST	"A Late Walk"	*127*
NORMA TILDEN	"The New Dog"	*128*
WISLAWA SZYMBORSKA	"True Love"	*130*
JOHN DONNE	"The Flea"	*132*
MATURAI ERUTTALAN CENTAMPUTAN	"What She Said"	*134*
GEORGIA DOUGLAS JOHNSON	"I Want to Die While You Love Me"	*135*
EDWIN MORGAN	"Strawberries"	*136*
BILLY COLLINS	"This Much I Do Remember"	*138*

Real Hope

WHEN YOU REDISCOVER YOURSELF AND YOUR STRENGTHS

CHIPPEWA MUSIC	"Sometimes I Go About Pitying Myself"	*151*
WILLIAM BUTLER YEATS	"The Lake Isle of Innisfree"	*152*
JANE HIRSHFIELD	"Da Capo"	*153*

KATE BINGHAM	"Home Sweet Home"	*154*
A. E. HOUSMAN	"Oh, When I Was in Love with You"	*156*
JANE KENYON	"In the Grove: The Poet at Ten"	*157*
HOWARD MOSS	"The Pruned Tree"	*158*
LOUISE GLÜCK	"Vespers"	*160*
ROBERT FROST	"To Earthward"	*162*
YEVGENY YEVTUSHENKO	"Lies"	*164*

Moving On

167

WHEN YOU REDISCOVER THE WORLD AND ITS JOYS

MARY OLIVER	"In Blackwater Woods"	*178*
ELIZABETH BISHOP	"The Fish"	*180*
JANE KENYON	"Let Evening Come"	*184*
BILLY COLLINS	"Morning"	*186*
W. H. AUDEN	"Musée des Beaux Arts"	*188*
MARK DOTY	"Tiara"	*190*
KIM KONOPKA	"Upon Entering"	*193*
DENISE LEVERTOV	"O Taste and See"	*194*
MAY SWENSON	"Strawberrying"	*195*
ROBERT MORGAN	"Honey"	*197*
ANNE MCNAUGHTON	"Teste Moanial"	*199*

CONTENTS

MIGUEL DE UNAMUNO   "Throw Yourself Like
                     Seed"   201
BILLY COLLINS   "Picnic, Lightning"   203
ROBERT FROST   "Mowing"   206
E. E. CUMMINGS   "i thank You God for
                     most this amazing"   207

Afterword   209
Biographies of Contributors   213
Acknowledgments   229
About the Editors   231

Introduction

*Parting is all we know of heaven
And all we need of hell.*

—EMILY DICKINSON

It was over. We were through, done, utterly broken up. After two years together, the guy I'd been dating—we'll call him Dick—had called it quits. I'm sure you can picture the scene. It wasn't pretty.

I raged, I cried, I defiantly faked being fine without him. I got really good at cursing, crying, smiling, and working all at the same time, and my colleagues got good at pretending not to notice. Life seemed absurd, meaningless. And it was all Dick's fault.

But, of course, it wasn't really.

It was up to me to get better, and I did. Wonderful friends and family pulled me out of the sadness. Leanne said, "Just remember that time I saw him wearing black socks with white tennis shoes." Rachel prodded, "Repeat this mantra: 'I do not fancy him, I do not fancy him.' God, he's horrid, how can you fancy him?" Elizabeth sighed, "You're being a self-absorbed ninny; read Doris Lessing and get back into teaching." I began to take more challenging freelance jobs, started teaching English again, reached out to people I'd been pushing away, immersed myself in the books and poems I loved again, rebuilt my core. I either didn't think about Dick, or I wanted him dead, or I wanted him back. It depended on the day, but all in all, I felt myself moving past the relationship.

More than anyone, Elizabeth helped me make my way through the hell of love. After thirty-two years of marriage, she knows a thing or two about it herself. We're both writers and teachers who believe in the transformative power of literature. I'm thirty-nine and a newlywed (married during the course of writing this book); Elizabeth is fifty-six and, as I said, the resident expert. Our relationship falls somewhere between sister-sister, mother-daughter, reader-writer, and best friends. We talk a lot about literature, life, and love, about how literature can bring the comfort, solace, and perspective that no therapist or self-help book can approach.

When I went to hell and back through my breakup with Dick, Elizabeth helped me find poems which became touchstones for me. They reminded me of who I was and who I wanted to be. Michael Fried's "Somewhere A Seed" allowed me to savor sweet revenge. William Butler Yeats's "The Lake Isle of Innisfree" gave me hope that I could create a happy home all by myself. Pablo Neruda's "If You Forget Me" let me indulge in melodramatic reconciliation fantasies. "The Art of Losing" and "The Fish" by Elizabeth Bishop convinced me that I had to master the art of losing if I ever wanted to get good at the art of living.

Elizabeth and I decided to write this book after watching friend after friend—women and men, gay and straight—experience wrenching breakups and divorces. We'd both spend hours with them, talking over coffee and on the phone, trying to provide support and comfort. Frequently we found ourselves offering these friends the consolation of literature—"Read this poem," we would say. "It will help." And sometimes it did.

Usually, though, we'd watch our friends grapple with new hair colors, new workout plans, new ways of determining who was from Mars and who was from Venus—whatever it took to distract them from the pain they felt. They often claimed that poetry seemed too remote and intimidating. But when we sat down with them and read a poem like Margaret Atwood's "you fit into me," they'd laugh. When we paraphrased Pablo Neruda's "If You Forget Me," they'd cry. These poems spoke to their experience, and convinced them that poetry wasn't all flowery fluff or incomprehensible babble. It was concrete. It filled an emptiness. They could carry poems with them like prayer books or stick them on the fridge as reminders. And they wanted more.

So we decided to create a book to help people survive a breakup—literary therapy for the brokenhearted. We put together a collection of "breakup poems," poems written by great writers, both classic and modern, from John Donne to Sandra Cisneros. Each section of the book represents the emotional stages we think people experience after a breakup. We begin with poems that express and dig into the anger, hurt, and depression of loss; then move to poems that ask why, analyze rifts, strive for explanation; and then poems that build resolve, envision a future, revel in the present.

But we didn't want to just throw a bunch of poems at readers and wish them good luck. That never quite worked for our friends. They only "got" the poems fully when we explained a line here or there, or pointed out an image and how it worked. So we've written brief introductions for each section in which we guide readers through the poems. We know that literature has the power to heal and transform all by itself—but we also know that sometimes people need help relating poetry to their own lives.

How *can* poetry help you through a breakup? Poet Mark Doty says:

> Being in grief, it turns out, is not unlike being in love. In both states, the imagination is entirely occupied with one person. . . . Everything that touches us seems to relate back to that center; there is no other emotional life, no place outside the universe of feeling centered on the pivotal figure.

If all roads lead back to the one you have lost, how do you know where to go now? You're still lost in love and in grief. There are no familiar landmarks; there is no firm ground under your feet. You know you're supposed to just move on into the future, but how do you get there? This collection is intended to provide a map for your broken heart, and each poem serves as a kind of compass, helping you find your real self (your true north) again. Think of it as a survival handbook, a guide to surviving love.

We know how much breakups hurt and how scary it is to risk love again. We understand the temptation to just say "The hell with love" and shut yourself off from new relationships. If you get back out in the world there's always the chance you'll be hurt again, of course. But there's also the chance that you'll find some peace and happiness. Or even better, that you'll have the opportunity to bring happiness to others. We think it's worth the effort, worth throwing yourself into the world and passionately pursuing love—not some idealized soul mate love of your life, but a more expansive, real love *of* life.

Ultimately, of course, it's your decision: stay in the hell of heartbreak, close yourself off from joy, and wait for something good to happen to you; or allow yourself to live fully in the earthly paradise of everyday existence. Risk life; risk love, as e.e. cummings urges in "i thank You God for most this amazing." Learn to be grateful for:

> *the leaping greenly spirits of trees*
> *and a blue true dream of a sky;*
> *and for everything*
> *which is natural which is infinite which*
> *is yes*

Rage

WHEN HATRED ISN'T STRONG ENOUGH

At least you know you're still alive—that's the one great thing about post-breakup anger. You want him to drop dead—well, maybe suffer some agonizing disfigurement first—and you can't say his name without spitting it and you want to slap every happy couple you see on the street. Not very pretty, but it beats being numb and limp. Rage gives you edge, keeps your blood pumping, gives you a reason to get up in the morning.

In fact, we live in a culture that encourages us to express our anger; doctors and therapists agree that repressed anger hurts our psyches and bodies. We're supposed to let it out. But raw, primal rage has its limits. So we smash every plate in the kitchen and rip up every last picture of him—all we're left with is a mess. Cathartic but not constructive.

That's where the "rage" poets come in. These artists have created tidy little arrangements of words, very controlled-looking, very civilized. Or so they seem. But each poem is a finely crafted bomb, packed with fury, vengefulness, and tremendous wit. To read one and "get it" is to experience an explosion of self-recognition—that *aha!* that makes you laugh and nod and marvel at how the words express exactly what you feel. You're not alone. In fact, you're in pretty eloquent company, which can make you feel a little better about being bitter.

Margaret Atwood's "you fit into me" shoots a pretty little bullet of rage, though at first glance it appears to be a tiny harmless love poem. "You fit into me," the speaker says, the way a hook on a door fits into the round eye of the latch, as if we hold each other together, we complete each other. Very domestic and sweet and sexual. But that romantic image flips in the second stanza— sure you fit into me, darling, like a fish hook stuck in my open eye. The combination of pain (there's a **#&#! hook stuck in my eye!) and calm self-awareness (my eyes were wide open but he hooked me anyway) make the poem a funny meditation on a really bad relationship.

"Somewhere A Seed," by Michael Fried, offers a similar surprise zinger of an ending. We vote this best poem to give someone in the first throes of breakup pain. The formal measured movement of the poem, its elegant structure (note that it's all one sentence), and the careful control in the speaker's voice lull you into thinking you're reading a conventional "there's growth and hope in Nature, so cheer up" kind of poem— unbearable when you've just been tossed aside by your one true love. Happily, "Seed" turns out to be a "someday, honey, you're going to suffer and die" kind of poem, a delicious, murderous revenge fantasy. The universe is a just place, the poem tells us, and will see to it that your ex gets his; someday, when he least expects it, that "shit-filled heart" of his will feel the kind of pain you're experiencing now.

It's somehow comforting to know that even the most classic, revered poets share this down-and-dirty impulse to see ex-lovers suffer. That's why we love John Donne's "The Message"—it makes a basic revenge impulse seem extraordinarily graceful and witty. What's more, it shows how a breakup victim can regain a bit of confidence and power through the controlled expression of anger.

In stanzas one and two of this poem, Donne's speaker assumes victim status—he wants his eyes back, "Which (Oh) too long have dwelt on thee." By the end of the stanza, however, he realizes that they are worthless, "Made by thee/fit for no good sight," so he changes his mind and decides he's better off without them. Next, he asks for his heart back—but later realizes it too has been corrupted by the lying ex-lover, "taught by thine/To make jestings/Of protestings." So he tells her to keep his eyes and his heart. In other words: I may not be able to recover from your betrayal—my vision will remain forever clouded, and my heart is broken for good.

But in stanza three, the speaker tires of being a victim and instead becomes inspired by anger. Wait a minute, he says, I've changed my mind again. "Send me back my heart and eyes," he demands—I'll need them so I can see you suffer when this happens to you, so that I "may laugh and joy, when thou/Art in anguish." It's a bitter kind of joy, but yes, hold on to your heart, says the poem, it will mend. Anger, oddly enough, may well be the first step toward recovery.

Louise Glück assures us that our anger is justifiable—there is reason, not just emotion, behind our rage. The speaker in "Unwritten Law" knows exactly why she is angry. For years she only dated "rather boyish men—unformed, sullen, or shyly kicking the dead leaves" because it was easy and she could keep her guard up and not risk too much of who she really was. But finally she fell for a man (not a boy) who made her feel a "true expansiveness, a buoyance and love of the earth," someone who took her "beyond the archetype" of all her past relationships. With him, she revealed everything, gave everything, and believed it was worth it; it was destiny. She "blessed [her] good fortune" in finding this man. And what was her reward for allowing herself to trust and believe and give thanks? He gradually (with smug cruelty) destroyed her faith in him, which destroyed her faith in good fortune (destiny, God), leaving her with meaninglessness. A bleak poem, but at least it's not just a cry of angry pain. She blames him but tries to accept her own responsibility for why she feels the way she does. There's a thought process here that explains the hurt and very well may help her move forward with her life.

Moving forward is what we ultimately want to do. One way to start is to acknowledge the anger and fantasize revenge, and then forgive yourself for feeling that way. You're allowed these feelings—you've lost so much, and you're so tired, disappointed, and wounded that you want someone else to hurt. It doesn't mean you're some *Fatal Attraction* wacko. Reveling in rage can give you the will to live again (there's a kind of giddy glee in imagining that arrow through his "shit-filled heart")—but clinging to anger only warps your own heart. You have to move beyond anger if you want to recover completely, that is, if you want to become a trusting, caring person again.

you fit into me

you fit into me
like a hook into an eye

a fish hook
an open eye

MARGARET ATWOOD

Somewhere A Seed

Somewhere a seed falls to the ground
That will become a tree
That will some day be felled
From which thin shafts will be extracted
To be made into arrows
To be fitted with warheads
One of which, some day when you least expect it,
While a winter sun is shining
On a river of ice
And you feel farthest from self-pity,
Will pierce your shit-filled heart.

MICHAEL FRIED

Hatred

I shall hate you
Like a dart of singing steel
Shot through still air
At even-tide.
Or solemnly
As pines are sober
When they stand etched
Against the sky.
Hating you shall be a game
Played with cool hands
And slim fingers.
Your heart will yearn
For the lonely splendor
Of the pine tree;
While rekindled fires
In my eyes
Shall wound you like swift arrows.
Memory will lay its hands
Upon your breast
And you will understand
My hatred.

GWENDOLYN BENNETT

The Message

Send home my long strayd eyes to mee,
Which (Oh) too long have dwelt on thee,
Yet since there they have learn'd such ill,
    Such forc'd fashions,
    And false passions,
      That they be
      Made by thee
Fit for no good sight, keep them still.

Send home my harmlesse heart againe,
Which no unworthy thought could staine,
Which if it be taught by thine
    To make jestings
    Of protestings,
      And breake both
      Word and oath,
Keepe it, for then 'tis none of mine.

Yet send me back my heart and eyes,
That I may know, and see thy lyes,
and may laugh and joy, when thou
    Art in anguish
    And dost languish
      For some one
      That will none,
Or prove as false as thou art now.

JOHN DONNE

Unwritten Law

Interesting how we fall in love:
in my case, absolutely. Absolutely, and,
      alas, often—
so it was in my youth.
And always with rather boyish men—
unformed, sullen, or shyly kicking the dead
      leaves:
in the manner of Balanchine.
Nor did I see them as versions of the same thing.
I, with my inflexible Platonism,
my fierce seeing of only one thing at a time:
I ruled against the indefinite article.
And yet, the mistakes of my youth
made me hopeless, because they repeated
      themselves,
as is commonly true.

But in you I felt something beyond the
        archetype—
a true expansiveness, a buoyance and love of
        the earth
utterly alien to my nature. To my credit,
I blessed my good fortune in you.
Blessed it absolutely, in the manner of those years.
And you in your wisdom and cruelty
gradually taught me the meaninglessness of
        that term.

LOUISE GLÜCK

Quick and Bitter

The end was quick and bitter.
Slow and sweet was the time between us,
slow and sweet were the nights
when my hands did not touch one another
        in despair
but with the love of your body
which came between them.

And when I entered into you
it seemed then that great happiness
could be measured with the precision
of sharp pain. Quick and bitter.

Slow and sweet were the nights.
Now is as bitter and grinding as sand—
"Let's be sensible" and similar curses.

And as we stray further from love
we multiply the words,
words and sentences long and orderly.
Had we remained together
we could have become a silence.

YEHUDA AMICHAI

Mock Orange

It is not the moon, I tell you.
It is these flowers
lighting the yard.

I hate them.
I hate them as I hate sex,
the man's mouth
sealing my mouth, the man's
paralyzing body—

and the cry that always escapes,
the low, humiliating
premise of union—

In my mind tonight
I hear the question and pursuing answer
fused in one sound
that mounts and mounts and then
is split into the old selves,
the tired antagonisms. Do you see?
We were made fools of.
And the scent of mock orange
drifts through the window.

How can I rest?
How can I be content
when there is still
that odor in the world?

LOUISE GLÜCK

wishes for sons

i wish them cramps.
i wish them a strange town
and the last tampon.
i wish them no 7-11.

i wish them one week early
and wearing a white skirt.
i wish them one week late.

later i wish them hot flashes
and clots like you
wouldn't believe. let the
flashes come when they
meet someone special.
let the clots come
when they want to.

let them think they have accepted
arrogance in the universe,
then bring them to gynecologists
not unlike themselves.

LUCILLE CLIFTON

Sadness

WHEN YOU'D RATHER DIE THAN EAT OR SLEEP

When you move from anger to sadness and despair, it's scary. You can't summon enough energy for anger, and you're so depressed that you can barely lift your head. Food either sickens you or you gorge on Cheetos and Dove bars. If you're not eating, you feel slack and wasted, and if you are eating everything in sight, you feel as if your flesh has turned to dough. You fall into a drugged haze of sleep; when you wake up at four A.M., you are gripped by sorrow and anxiety. Washing your face (never mind your hair) is barely worth the effort, and there is no one around to notice that you've been wearing the same filthy sweatpants for weeks.

Perhaps the most difficult and frightening part of this spiraling depression is the struggle to keep some small part of yourself alive enough to know that this feeling will end, that yes, you will dig your way out of this black hole and find your whole self—and the world—again.

And we understand if you are thinking that poetry is the last thing you need. But here's how it helps: These poets have articulated their sadness; they have risen from their chairs and beds and TV sets to sort and sift and frame their feelings. Reading these poems and connecting with them lets you know that others have felt the same bleak despair and have turned that feeling into poems. And even if you read these poems flat on your back, a nod or a sigh of recognition might begin to lift you from the horrible inertia of depression.

In "Solitary Observation Brought Back from a Sojourn in Hell" and "After Great Pain," Louise Bogan and Emily Dickinson offer us a way to shape and focus our pain. For Bogan, the title tells all: I was alone in hell—now I'm back and here's what I learned. She then distills our misery to seven words that artfully sum up the present hell of our lives. The poem even contains a whisper of hope; she came back from hell. Like Bogan, Dickinson (for whom, we imagine, there were no sweats or Dove bars allowed, just a straight-backed chair and a writing table in the sitting room) provides shape for our pain. In "After Great Pain" she perfectly describes the leadenness of depression: "This is the Hour of Lead." If we can function at all—our mechanical feet go "a Wooden way"—we have become inert, dead, like stone. But like Bogan, Dickinson suggests that even after "the chill, the stupor," and the letting go, it is possible to outlive and survive great pain.

Billy Collins, in "Some Days," also shows us a world where we are stripped of our humanity. No longer little girls playing with dolls, we have become the dolls, powerless, "lifted up by the ribs," and "staring straight ahead" with our "little plastic faces." When our hearts are broken, we do feel as if we're made of plastic—fixed and frozen—when before, when perfectly in love, we were "striding around like vivid gods," our "shoulders in the clouds." And yet Collins reminds us in the title, it really is only "some days" that we feel at the mercy of some giant, malicious child. On all of the other days, even if we are no longer gods, we are human, and our powers are intact.

We've included William Carlos Williams's "The Widow's Lament in Springtime" and Joseph Stroud's "The Song of Divorce" because even though your friends may tell you that it's "only" a breakup, the loss feels as final as death or divorce. And both of these poets tell us that the beauty of the natural world does not necessarily make our loss easier to bear. When we are in pain, the warmth of sunlight and the splendor of spring are a slap in the face. Williams's widow knows that springtime is the worst time because the world refuses to match her mood; "The plumtree is white today/with masses of flowers," but she wants only to fall and sink into them. For Stroud, everything that was sweet has turned bitter— sunlight, moonlight, even the memories that we thought we'd have forever. We believe that these poems help just a bit, because no matter how your friends insist that it will do you good to get up and take a walk, they're wrong, you'll probably feel worse. Both of these poems give you permission to feel rotten on a glorious, sunlit day.

Larry Vélez, in "Chinese Dragons," and James Wright, in "Lying in a Hammock at William

Duffy's Farm in Pine Island, Minnesota," agree; you can feel terrible anywhere—in the city or the country. The darkness, for a while anyway, is inescapable. For Vélez, it's in the subway, "sleek, metallic snakes" filled with unseeing people who dissolve and disengage. He warns against thinking that the country is any better: it is all "mud and horseshit" where we walk "like crippled crows." Wright is of the same mind: a hammock at a friend's farm filled with bronze butterflies and green shadows will not necessarily heal your wounds. Sunlight may briefly turn that horseshit to "golden stones," but when evening comes, we are left with plain old horseshit.

"I have wasted my life," Wright concludes. But hold on, it's not as bleak as it sounds. It may actually be liberating to hang motionless for a while, watching the world move in its seemingly heartless cycles. You've lost the person you love, and with that your sense of purpose and beauty and joy. So lie there and feel your loss—and in doing so, become part of the cycle, too: afternoon to evening to morning again. Maybe tomorrow you'll focus more on the sunlight than the horseshit. And like the speaker (and so many of our poets), we're allowed to defy magnificent nature, to say, "Yes, there's sunlight, and green shadow, and bronze butterflies, but so what? I've wasted my life anyway. (But maybe I'll just get up, have a latte, and check my e-mail.)"

It hurts, Marilyn Hacker says, this feeling of loss and darkness and pain—it's every kind of ache, "stomach, head, and heart." In this excerpt from "Coda," she suggests a profound absence of sunlight: "The winter evenings drift dark to the window." We find little comfort as she invites us to mourn "for the dead chances, for the end of being young." And John Ash, in "Cigarettes," offers even less comfort. Our great passion, this grand love affair, is like a cigarette that has filled all our empty spaces, but once it has burned down, we are left only with "whatever trash may be at hand." Even worse, the passion itself may be malignant. What if we never recover? Ash articulates our very deepest, darkest fear: what if we die alone in "an anonymous hotel or hospital, under the blank gaze of a washstand, a bad painting or an empty vase"? Then again, perhaps the therapists are right, and we can't begin to feel better until we *do* face our worst fears.

In brief speeches from *Hamlet* and *Macbeth*, William Shakespeare describes the moment-to-moment, day-in-day-out feelings of awfulness that come from contemplating these fears. Says Hamlet (ultimate breakup for him—his mom has just married his uncle), "O God! God!/How weary, stale, flat, and unprofitable,/Seem to me all the uses of this world!/Fie on't, ah fie!" Yes, all of life seems to have lost its savor—the world is "rank and gross in nature." And he's right, our very flesh seems to have turned against us—we've lost the gift of living comfortably in our own skins. We are rank and gross. And everything—work, friendship, and especially love—has been proven to be stale and flat. *Macbeth* only deepens our misery—our entire lives are pointless. (Breakup for him? Lady Macbeth, the only one who could share the depth of his woes, has just died.) Life is "a poor player" that "struts and frets his hour upon the stage." We are reminded of empty days of shopping—artfully arranging our newest acquisitions from Pottery Barn, posing, strutting, and fretting through Barney's and Bloomingdale's. Yes, says Shakespeare, all of it is meaningless; "It is a tale/Told by an idiot, full of sound and fury, Signifying nothing."

So thanks a lot, you say, this is supposed to make me feel better? Look, Hamlet was a prince, Macbeth a king—for a brief time, you get to be the queen of your own Shakespearean drama. Revel in it, read these speeches out loud, scream "Fie on't! O fie!" until your upstairs neighbor pounds on the floor—and then get thee to a video store, rent *Shakespeare in Love*. We believe you will begin to see what Shakespeare tells us: to be fully human we must feel this kind of pain. In his autobiography, William Butler Yeats says, "We begin to live when we have conceived life as a tragedy." So yes, you've had your bit of tragedy, and you *will* begin to live and feel things more deeply, including love when it comes again.

Solitary Observation Brought Back from a Sojourn in Hell

At midnight tears
Run into your ears.

LOUISE BOGAN

After Great Pain

After great pain, a formal feeling comes—
The Nerves sit ceremonious, like Tombs—
The stiff Heart questions was it He, that bore,
And Yesterday, or Centuries before?

The Feet, mechanical, go round—
Of Ground, or Air, or Ought—
A Wooden way
Regardless grown,
A Quartz contentment, like a stone—

This is the Hour of Lead—
Remembered, if outlived,
As Freezing persons, recollect the Snow—
First—Chill—then Stupor—then the letting go—

EMILY DICKINSON

Some Days

Some days I put the people in their places at
    the table,
bend their legs at the knees,
if they come with that feature,
and fix them into the tiny wooden chairs.

All afternoon they face one another,
the man in the brown suit,
the woman in the blue dress,
perfectly motionless, perfectly behaved.

But other days, I am the one
who is lifted up by the ribs,
then lowered into the dining room of a dollhouse
to sit with the others at the long table.

Very funny,
but how would you like it
if you never knew from one day to the next
if you were going to spend it

striding around like a vivid god,
your shoulders in the clouds
or sitting down there amidst the wallpaper,
staring straight ahead with your little plastic face?

BILLY COLLINS

The Widow's Lament in Springtime

Sorrow is my own yard
where the new grass
flames as it has flamed
often before but not
with the cold fire
that closes round me this year.
Thirtyfive years
I lived with my husband.
The plumtree is white today
with masses of flowers.
Masses of flowers
load the cherry branches
and color some bushes
yellow and some red
but the grief in my heart
is stronger than they
for though they were my joy
formerly, today I notice them
and turned away forgetting.

Today my son told me
that in the meadows,
at the edge of the heavy woods
in the distance, he saw
trees of white flowers.
I feel that I would like
to go there
and fall into those flowers
and sink into the marsh near them.

WILLIAM CARLOS WILLIAMS

The Song of Divorce

Bitter the warmth of sunlight, and bitter the
    taste of apple,
the song and the stars and wheat fields, bitter
    the memory,
moonlight, the shine of the lake's surface
    in morning
like a sheen of pearl, bitter the hummingbird's
    throat
and gold pollen, all poems and their music,
    harp wood
and sandalwood, *bitter,* silk sheets, fire,
    the marriage.

JOSEPH STROUD

Chinese Dragons

The immature elm wears a rustcolored vest.
I have found my way from her basement address
to the rest of my life in the city.
Beneath the street dragon's teeth
delete the space
between the first and the last.

Sleek, metallic snakes
slide beneath our cities,
shrieking as our reading,
unseeing people
dissolve and disengage.

We are not pleased
to see the rats and the roaches,
the derelicts who dare
to pluck our deafened souls
with songs so badly sung
we are relieved to purchase
silence, never mind
"Thank you."

Their hairy bodies stink.
Their sooty fingers remind us of the pale roots
we sometimes have to chop
off dusty brown potatoes,
and cornsilk,
and plowed fields.
The mud and horseshit
stick to boots until we walk
like crippled crows
up to the mudporch,
cursing all horses
and allnight rain,
slapping at the dogs,
hooting at the bleached moon hanging
low over the looming elms
filled with starlings
on their way to someplace else.

LARRY VÉLEZ

Lying in a Hammock at William Duffy's Farm in Pine Island, Minnesota

Over my head, I see the bronze butterfly,
Asleep on the black trunk,
Blowing like a leaf in green shadow.
Down the ravine behind the empty house,
The cowbells follow one another
Into the distances of the afternoon.
To my right,
In a field of sunlight between two pines,
The droppings of last year's horses
Blaze up into golden stones.
I lean back, as the evening darkens and comes on.
A chicken hawk floats over, looking for home.
I have wasted my life.

JAMES WRIGHT

From "Coda"

Did you love well what very soon you left?
Come home and take me in your arms and take
away this stomach ache, headache, heartache.
Never so full, I never was bereft
so utterly. The winter evenings drift
dark to the window. Not one work will make
you, where you are, turn in your day, or wake
from your night toward me. The only gift
I got to keep or give is what I've cried,
floodgates let down to mourning for the dead
chances, for the end of being young,
for everyone I loved who really died.
I drank our one year out in brine instead
of honey from the seasons of your tongue.

MARILYN HACKER

Cigarettes

Problems of translation are, perhaps, not so great
between languages, as between different versions
of the same language. Why, for example, does
"fag" mean homosexual in America, when,
in England, it means cigarette? Does this imply
that those who first observed the phenomenon
of smoking in the New World were homosexual?
This would cause some consternation on
        Columbus Day,
and, in all likelihood, the assumption is
        unjustified,
since Columbus and his crew were not
        English-speakers.

Yet, if we dismiss the idea of happy crowds of
homosexual Spanish or Italian mariners
returning to Europe with cigarettes in hand,
eager to introduce this new pleasure to their
      lovers,
we should perhaps concede that there is some
      connection
between the two ideas. It was Oscar Wilde,
      after all,
who described smoking as "the perfect pleasure,
      because"—
he opined—"it always leaves one unsatisfied."
It is clear from this that he was thinking of
      sexual pleasure,
of the working-class youths with whom he so
      recklessly dined
in fashionable restaurants of the eighteen
      nineties.
A cigarette is like a passion in that it is inhaled
      deeply
and seems to fill all the empty spaces of the body,
until, of course, it burns down, and is put out amid
the shells of pistachio nuts, or whatever trash
may be at hand, and the passion may leave traces

that in time will grow malignant: he who has
      taken pleasure
may die many years after in the room of an
      anonymous
hotel or hospital, under the blank gaze of a
      washstand,
a bad painting or an empty vase, having
      forgotten entirely
the moment that announced the commencement
of his dying. And perhaps he will not understand:
it is another false translation, like someone
      stumbling over
the word for cigarette in a new and intolerable
      language.

JOHN ASH

Hamlet
(Act I, sc. 2, lines 129–137)

O! that this too too sullied flesh would melt,
Thaw and resolve itself into a dew!
Or that the Everlasting had not fix'd
His canon 'gainst self-slaughter! O God! God!
How weary, stale, flat, and unprofitable,
Seem to me all the uses of this world!
Fie on 't! ah fie! 'tis an unweeded garden,
That grows to seed; things rank and gross
    in nature
Possess it merely.

WILLIAM SHAKESPEARE

Macbeth
(Act V, sc. 5, lines 19–28)

Tomorrow, and tomorrow, and tomorrow,
Creeps in this petty pace from day to day
To the last syllable of recorded time,
And all our yesterdays have lighted fools
The way to dusty death. Out, out, brief candle!
Life's but a walking shadow, a poor player
That struts and frets his hour upon the stage
And then is heard no more: it is a tale
Told by an idiot, full of sound and fury,
Signifying nothing.

WILLIAM SHAKESPEARE

Self~Hatred

WHEN YOU'RE CONVINCED IT'S ALL YOUR FAULT

So you've raged and ranted and cried when you heard that song or walked down that block or smelled the shirt he left at your place. Now you're trying to pull yourself together. Feel a little less, think a little more. I can get over this, you say. I can get over this, I can get over this.

But it's hard to get past the big WHY. Why did it happen? How could it have happened? Your friends remind you that it's because he said you had a moustache or he cheated with the au pair down the street or he said he could never be with a woman who didn't like jazz. In short, he made you feel you weren't pretty, thin, or smart enough. You know they're right—it's better that it's over. Healthier, they say. And you want to be healthy. You want to stop the anger and the tears.

Still, deep down you can't quite believe it was all his fault. He never would have left if only you'd been more tolerant, or tougher, or a better communicator, or less of a nag. If only you'd figured out the right balance of who or what to be, you'd still have him, you think. (What's more, you *do* have a bit of a moustache and you don't know Miles Davis from Metallica.) You can't tell your friends this because they'll throw up their hands and tell you to see a shrink. So you keep it inside and let it eat you up.

And that's when you slip into one of the worst stages of post-breakup hell: Self-Hatred. Not a stage we exactly embrace, but plenty of us go through it in a big way. The speaker in Louise Bogan's "Women," for example, doesn't just hate herself, she condemns her whole gender. Women! she sniffs. We sit around waiting for life to happen, while men get out in the world. Like cowboys, they roam the range of their dreams and ambitions; they see "cattle cropping red winter grass" and "snow water going down under culverts." We weeny women, on the other hand, hang out in the "tight hot cell of [our] hearts" starving ourselves on the "dusty bread" of old someday-my-prince-will-come dreams. Life—

and maybe love—passes us by because we let it, she says. And maybe because we deserve it—there's a strong element of punishment in self-hatred. I screwed up, you think, so I'd better teach myself a lesson.

Okay, fine, you might think in the self-hatred stage, fine, I'll just lock away my dreams of true love and passion and creative partnership and domestic bliss. I'm not worthy of them. That's the conscious choice of the speaker in Gwendolyn Brooks's "my dreams, my works, must wait till after hell." She decides to hold her honey and store her bread (her femininity, her dreams and desires) until she returns from the hell of heartbreak. She's hungry for love, but she refuses to open herself to anyone; she "keep[s] eyes pointed in." What's surprising and poignant about this poem, though, is that the speaker sees some hope for herself. Someday, when "the devil days of . . . hurt/Drag out to their last dregs," she'll go home to her old pure self, where she'll take out, and love again, her very own honey and bread.

Purity, the speaker wants. So much of self-hatred comes from feeling used up, corrupted, tainted. We want to be as clear-eyed and clean, as loving and lovable as we were when we were little girls. While we can never fully bring back that kind of innocence, we can move a little closer to it by trying to accept ourselves for who we are. A little battered and a little tired, but not the monsters we imagine ourselves to be.

Easier said than done, of course. The speaker in Sandra Cisneros's "The Heart Rounds Up the Usual Suspects" sees herself as "a pathetic bitch" who sleeps with anyone who will give her a sign of affection. Like the speaker in the Bogan poem, she hates not just herself, but all women—for being so needy, like stray cats, who are "grateful to excessiveness" when a man (even a "cyclop") takes them in. She wants to be hard on herself for this self-loathing behavior, as if she deserves it, but at the same time she seems to be asking and hoping for salvation from herself. "Have you seen this woman?" she asks. She is "armed and dangerous." Stop her from hating and hurting herself.

We hate to admit it, but self-hatred is one of the hardest stages to shake after a breakup. Sometimes our superficial efforts to move past it only make things worse, as Steve Kowit's "Cosmetics Do No Good" shows. The poem is so terribly honest about that "put on a happy—or at least artificially enhanced—face" approach we bravely try when we're making ourselves date and socialize again. "Cosmetics do no good," the speaker tells us. "My loveliness is past/& no one could be more aware than I am/that coquettish-ness at this age/only renders me ridiculous." We *do* feel ridiculous, and resentful, that we have to get out there and try to be pretty, seductive women when we feel like last week's baloney sandwich. But we try anyway, risk humiliation, because we desperately want renewal (just as we crave that old purity). Even though we only feel ruin now, we live in hope of salvation.

So we put on our game faces and wait for deliverance from our misery. Then a month goes by, and nothing has happened. No prince has swooped in for the rescue, even though we've whitened our teeth and highlighted our hair. The temptation at this point is to give up, retreat from social life, stop trying to look even slightly attrac-tive. No one wants me anyway, you think, so I'm going to sit at home and dwell on all the reasons why I'm disgusting and wretched. First, you decide to blame society, like the speaker in Marge Piercy's "A Work of Artifice." Society wants to keep women "small and cozy,/domestic and weak," just like little bonsai trees. And women fall for it. They physically prune themselves (diets, waxing, liposuction), sacrificing emotional and intellectual growth in pursuit of some feminine fantasy. I could have "grown eighty feet tall/on the side of a mountain," you think, if I just hadn't bought into the whole gotta-make-Prince-Charming-want-me routine. Now here I am with my "crippled brain," stuck in this stupid "attractive pot" of an apartment for the rest of my life.

Of course, if only your parents had raised you differently, none of this would've happened—the societal brainwashing, the doomed romance, the now garishly highlighted hair. Right, it's *their* fault you hate yourself, you decide next. They were too hard on you, or too lax, or too happy or too miserable. Like the speaker in Sharon Olds's "I Go Back to May 1937," you want to rush back to the time before they got together and scream, "Stop,/don't do it—she's the wrong woman,/he's the wrong man . . . /you are going to do bad things to children." To some extent, you *do* need to look back at who you are and what has shaped you. A little critical self-reflection (guided by a good therapist) can go a long way toward helping you like yourself again. But if you can, try to keep the whole "I'm the victim of a messed-up family" factor in perspective. Every family has its issues, as your parents' families did, and their parents' families before them. Being the product of a dysfunctional family has become the norm, and there's something absurdly funny about that, which is why we love Philip Larkin's "This Be the Verse." It's a potty-mouthed nursery rhyme, a Dr. Seuss–like romp of a poem that may just help you laugh your way out of self-hatred.

And you've got to pull yourself out somehow—we've seen people spiral into self-hatred that lasts for years. If you're not careful, it can become your identity and your favorite pastime—you fashion yourself as the jaded, scorned woman who mocks herself and everyone around her. That pose may seem safer than risking love again, but we think it's far more dangerous. Self-destruction feeds on self-hatred. You don't want to be like the speaker in Joseph Stroud's "Memories at the Movies." Stuck in the movie theater, watching a film he paid to see, he cowers from a disgustingly graphic scene—a vulture devouring a buffalo carcass, up to its neck in the asshole, "ripping and gulping bits of entrails." It dawns on the speaker that he is his own vulture, feeding on a dead relationship, his "head plunged into memories" of lost love. If he continues "tearing and feasting on the past," he'll wind up like the buffalo carcass, "cleaned out, gutted, empty inside."

Blech. We hope we've grossed you out of self-hatred. Come back to the living, to what's before you now and what lies ahead. The relationship went bad for all sorts of reasons, not because you're a screwup. Take responsibility for your part, and then let it go. You were many wonderful things to many people before you met him— don't let this one event define who you are. Ease up, look forward, and let yourself like yourself again.

Women

Women have no wilderness in them,
They are provident instead,
Content in the tight hot cell of their hearts
To eat dusty bread.

They do not see cattle cropping red winter grass,
They do not hear
Snow water going down under culverts
Shallow and clear.

They wait, when they should turn to journeys,
They stiffen, when they should bend.
They use against themselves that benevolence
To which no man is friend.

They cannot think of so many crops to a field
Or of clean wood cleft by an axe.
Their love is an eager meaninglessness
Too tense, or too lax.

They hear in every whisper that speaks to them
A shout and a cry.
As like as not, when they take life over their
      door-sills
They should let it go by.

LOUISE BOGAN

my dreams, my works, must wait till after hell

I hold my honey and I store my bread
In little jars and cabinets of my will.
I label clearly, and each latch and lid
I bid, Be firm till I return from hell.
I am very hungry. I am incomplete.
And none can tell when I may dine again.
No man can give me any word but Wait,
The puny light. I keep eyes pointed in;
Hoping that, when the devil days of my hurt
Drag out to their last dregs and I resume
On such legs as are left me, in such heart
As I can manage, remember to go home,
My taste will not have turned insensitive
To honey and bread old purity could love.

GWENDOLYN BROOKS

The Heart Rounds Up
the Usual Suspects

I sleep with the cat
when no one will have me.
When I can't give it away
for love or money—

I telephone the ones
who used to love me.
Or try to lure the leery
into my pretty web.

I'm loony as a June bride.
Cold as a *bruja*'s tit.
A pathetic bitch.
In short, an ordinary woman.
Grateful to excessiveness.

At the slightest tug of generousness,
I stick to the cyclop who takes me,
lets me pee on the carpet
and keeps me fed.

Have you seen this woman?
I am considered harmless.
Armed and dangerous.
But only to me.

SANDRA CISNEROS

Cosmetics Do No Good

Cosmetics do no good:
no shadow, rouge, mascara, lipstick—
nothing helps.
However artfully I comb my hair,
embellishing my throat & wrist with jewels,
it is no use—there is no
semblance of the beautiful young girl
I was
& long for still.
My loveliness is past.
& no one could be more aware than I am
that coquettishness at this age
only renders me ridiculous.

I know it. Nevertheless,
I primp myself before the glass
like an infatuated schoolgirl
fussing over every detail,
practicing whatever subtlety
may please him.
I cannot help myself.
The God of Passion has his will of me
& I am tossed about
between humiliation and desire,
rectitude & lust,
disintegration & renewal,
ruin & salvation.

STEVE KOWIT

A Work of Artifice

The bonsai tree
in the attractive pot
could have grown eighty feet tall
on the side of a mountain
till split by lightning.
But a gardener
carefully pruned it.
It is nine inches high.
Every day as he
whittles back the branches
the gardener croons,
It is your nature
to be small and cozy,
domestic and weak;
how lucky, little tree,
to have a pot to grow in.

With living creatures
one must begin very early
to dwarf their growth:
the bound feet,
the crippled brain,
the hair in curlers,
the hands you
love to touch.

MARGE PIERCY

I Go Back to May 1937

I see them standing at the formal gates of their
        colleges,
I see my father strolling out
under the ochre sandstone arch, the
red tiles glinting like bent
plates of blood behind his head, I
see my mother with a few light books at her hip
standing at the pillar made of tiny bricks with the
wrought-iron gate still open behind her, its
sword-tips black in the May air,
they are about to graduate, they are about to
        get married,
they are kids, they are dumb, all they know is
        they are
innocent, they would never hurt anybody.

I want to go up to them and say Stop,
don't do it—she's the wrong woman,
he's the wrong man, you are going to do things
you cannot imagine you would ever do,
you are going to do bad things to children,
you are going to suffer in ways you never heard of,
you are going to want to die. I want to go
up to them there in the late May sunlight and
        say it,
her hungry pretty blank face turning to me,
her pitiful beautiful untouched body,
his arrogant handsome blind face turning to me,
his pitiful beautiful untouched body,
but I don't do it. I want to live. I
take them up like the male and female
paper dolls and bang them together
at the hips like chips of flint as if to
strike sparks from them, I say
Do what you are going to do, and I will tell
        about it.

SHARON OLDS

69

This Be the Verse

They fuck you up, your mum and dad.
They may not mean to, but they do.
They fill you with the faults they had
And add some extra, just for you.

But they were fucked up in their turn
By fools in old-style hats and coats,
Who half the time were soppy-stern
And half at one another's throats.

Man hands on misery to man.
It deepens like a coastal shelf.
Get out as early as you can,
And don't have any kids yourself.

PHILIP LARKIN

Memories at the Movies

Malle's *Phantom India* makes you look at the
      vulture
feeding on the buffalo carcass, its featherless
fleshy neck smeared with blood, the entire screen
an image of curved hooking beak, ripping
and gulping bits of entrails. You look away,
cover your eyes, hoping the scene will change.
When you glance again, there's the bloated corpse
and flies and greedy inflamed eye of the buzzard
which now plunges its whole head and neck
into the buffalo's asshole, picking out coils
      of intestine.
The camera doesn't move, the film continues
      to scroll.
Eventually you have to look, you've *paid*
to see this mess, but the more you look the less
distant it is—the deeper into it, the more
      it becomes
un-ugly, becomes just bird feeding on body,
until you're cleaned out, gutted, empty inside
      yourself,

fighting back all those memories of her,
of being in this same theater, shoulder
to shoulder in the dark, deep into *Les Enfants
du Paradis*, *Jules et Jim*—all unreeled at last now,
the film coiling on the projection floor as you sit
in the present with your head plunged
into memories, the way love will leave you,
unspooled, the way you become your own vulture
tearing and feasting on the past.

JOSEPH STROUD

False Hope

WHEN YOU'RE CONVINCED YOU CAN GET BACK TOGETHER

So you've moved from senseless rage to speechless sorrow to relentless self-hatred, and let's face it, you're exhausted. All of that probing the past has left you desperate for respite. You're ready to give yourself a break, to peek out at the world again with a tiny sense of hope.

We're all for hope—as long as it's real. What's dangerous at this point is false hope, the kind that has you saying on the outside, "Okay, folks, move along, nothing to look at here. This wreck's all cleaned up," but obsessing on the inside, "We're gonna get back together, we're gonna get back together." You've got this little manic idea buzzing in your head, this stubborn belief that no matter what your friends and your therapist say, you and your ex are absolutely meant for each other in a soul mate kind of way. There's comfort in this belief, as if you have secret knowledge of what deep, true love really is, and therefore you're immune to the kind of breakups mere mortals experience. Your ex still burns for you somewhere, somehow, and just knowing this gives you the desire to live again.

We call this good hope gone bad, big time. And there's no easy way out, because snapping out of it means ending the fantasy that you still own his heart. We really hate this fragile stage, when you're like a broken window that's been taped back together, poised to crash back to the floor as soon as the wind blows. You convince yourself you're good as new when in fact you're still a mass of shards. It's so horribly pathetic and yet so brave at the same time.

Take the speaker in Pablo Neruda's "If You Forget Me," for example. Her lover is on his way out of their relationship, but she simply cannot face that truth. So she seesaws between fake "I don't need you" tough talk and "Please say you love me" desperation. It's obvious that she loves this guy madly—everything makes her long for him, everything she smells, sees, and touches. So when she tries to pretend that she'll be just fine without him—well, her childish bravado makes us cringe. "If suddenly/you forget me/do not look for me,/for I shall already have forgotten you," she declares, and if you "decide to leave me," then "I shall lift my arms/and my roots will set off/to seek another land." Talk about empty threats. She's just trying to defend herself against the devastating possibility that this man who is her entire existence no longer loves her. Meanwhile, she lives on the hope that he waits for her somewhere, that "each day, each hour" he feels that he is "destined for [her] with implacable sweetness."

The really sad thing about this kind of false hope is the instability of it all, the insecurity that comes from letting your whole life hang on an *if* proposition. If he still loves me, you tell yourself, then I wasn't wrong and I wasn't rejected; I can trust my instincts, God, and the universe again, because hope lives in that *if*. What you don't see is that you're powerless in this situation, completely dependent on the other person (and your own delusions) for your happiness.

And who wouldn't prefer blissful delusion to the reality of loss? False hope is like morphine for our breakup pain. If we could will ourselves to stop hurting, we'd do it, but it hurts too damn much to attempt it cold turkey.

Look at the speaker in Michael Drayton's "Since There's No Help." He tries to act nonchalant about the breakup, happy even ("And I am glad, yea, glad with all my heart/That thus so cleanly I myself can free") for the first half of the poem. But the second half reveals his utter heartbreak. You're killing Love, he tells his ex, and dragging down Passion, Faith, and Innocence, all that is pure and true and good. Don't do it, he begs. Perform a miracle instead, because you're the only one who can. Get back together with me, and in doing so bring Love back to life.

The speaker in Coventry Patmore's "A Farewell" starts off with a similar stoicism. I accept that we have to part ways for good, he tells his lover, and I won't try to fool myself into believing we'll ever get back together. You go East, I'll go West, and that's that, unless . . . maybe this isn't the end. Maybe someday we'll come "full circle" and find each other again—yeah, that's the ticket! Did I say good-bye? I meant, Hello, we're going to be together forever! This farewell becomes a reunion fantasy, complete with happy "tears of recognition."

Are you seeing a pattern here? We do, and it scares the pants off of us. In False Hope, you're so close to moving past the hurt, to getting your life back, but you keep looking backward, remembering only some Harlequin version of your relationship. So you set yourself up for hurt again and again. We know people who've spent *years* in False Hope Land. Don't let it happen to you.

Use the fates of Elvis Presley and Emma Bovary as cautionary tales, if it helps. Both Elvis and Emma (heroine of Gustave Flaubert's *Madame Bovary*) recklessly pursued idealized notions of romance—they gorged on "gilt and glitz," and fantasies of what love was supposed to be. What did it get them? Heartbreak hotels, where they both wound up, "wracked and ruined."

If you're going to delude yourself, at least do it consciously, if that's possible. Decide, like the speaker in Juana Inés de la Cruz's "I Can't Hold

You and I Can't Leave You," that you're going to indulge in a bit of "make believe" for a while. Half of you will "always be armed to abhor" your ex, and the other half will stand "ready to adore" him. You're ambivalent for now, half in hate and half in love, and that's okay. At least you're aware.

Or try this. Let yourself fantasize a little, remember the sweetest parts of the relationship, but then make yourself remember the rest, too. That's what the speaker in Carolyn Creedon's killer poem "litany" does. She knows she's being childish and unrealistic when she asks Tom over and over for things she knows he won't give her, but she asks anyway, the way people pray when they know the end is near (a litany is a prayer, after all). She asks him to love her, help her, father her children, comfort her, become her sun and her god, someone who will "baptise [her] with sex and cool water." But Tom is no god; he's just a guy. He can offer her tenderness and easy charm (which make her love him all the more) and increasingly brutal honesty. Yes, he'll have sex with her, but no, he won't be with her in public, and no, he won't stay with her. And at the end of the poem, when she asks, "How will I know how you love me?" he responds, "i have left you. that is how you will know." And she does know. That's what pushes the speaker just beyond false hope. She sees the limits and the finality of the relationship. Tom is gone, and there is no love to hold on to.

Somehow Creedon and our False Hope poets make it okay, even brave and beautiful, to expose our shattered hearts in False Hope. Your hope for reconciliation may be false, they seem to say, but the love driving you to cling to that hope is true and pure. Drop the delusions, but hang on to the part of you that is able to love fiercely. In the end, that's what will pull you through.

If You Forget Me

I want you to know
one thing.

You know how this is:
if I look
at the crystal moon, at the red branch
of the slow autumn at my window,
if I touch
near the fire
the impalpable ash
or the wrinkled body of the log,
everything carries me to you,
as if everything that exists,
aromas, light, metals,
were little boats that sail
toward those isles of yours that wait for me.

Well, now,
if little by little you stop loving me
I shall stop loving you little by little.

If suddenly
you forget me
do not look for me,
for I shall already have forgotten you.

If you think it long and mad,
the wind of banners
that passes through my life,
and you decide
to leave me at the shore
of the heart where I have roots,
remember
that on that day,
at that hour,
I shall lift my arms
and my roots will set off
to seek another land.

But
if each day,
each hour,
you feel that you are destined for me
with implacable sweetness,
if each day a flower
climbs up to your lips to seek me,
ah my love, ah my own,
in me all that fire is repeated,
in me nothing is extinguished or forgotten,
my love feeds on your love, beloved,
and as long as you live it will be in your arms
without leaving mine.

PABLO NERUDA

The Vow

When the lover
goes, the vow though
broken remains, that
trace of eternity love
brings down among us
stays, to give
dignity to the suffering
and to intensify it.

GALWAY KINNELL

Since There's No Help

Since there's no help, come let us kiss and part—
Nay, I have done, you get no more of me;
And I am glad, yea glad with all my heart,
That thus so cleanly I myself can free;
Shake hands forever, cancel all our vows,
And when we meet at any time again,
Be it not seen in either of our brows
That we one jot of former love retain.
Now at the last gasp of Love's latest breath,
When, his pulse failing, Passion speechless lies,
When Faith is kneeling by his bed of death,
And Innocence is closing up his eyes,
　　—Now if thou would'st when all have given
　　　　him over,
　　From death to life thou might'st him yet recover.

MICHAEL DRAYTON

A Farewell

With all my will, but much against my heart,
We two now part.
My Very Dear,
Our solace is, the sad road lies so clear.
It needs no art,
With faint, averted feet
And many a tear,
In our opposed paths to persevere.
Go thou to East, I West.
We will not say
There's any hope, it is so far away.

But, O, my Best,
When the one darling of our widowhead,
The nursling Grief,
Is dead,
And no dews blur our eyes
To see the peach-bloom come in evening skies,
Perchance we may,
Where now this night is day,
And even through faith of still averted feet,
Making full circle of our banishment,
Amazed meet;
The bitter journey to the bourne so sweet
Seasoning the termless feast of our content
With tears of recognition never dry.

COVENTRY PATMORE

Elvis P. and Emma B.

Bear with me:
Memphis is not far
from Yonville-L'Abbaye,
and would you have guessed
at the cornfields, blond,
set against a tidy French sky
and a wilder Tennessee one?

Elvis and Emma
went in for spending
were Philistines
were suckers
for gilt and glitz
were wracked and ruined
by Romance.

Monsieur Lheureux and
Colonel Parker
were fat and happy.

We knew from the beginning
that the Hotel-de-Boulogne,
as well as any Hilton,
was full of heartbreak.

ELIZABETH ASH VÉLEZ

I Can't Hold You and
I Can't Leave You

I can't hold you and I can't leave you,
and sorting the reasons to leave you or hold you,
I find an intangible one to love you,
and many tangible ones to forgo you.

As you won't change, nor let me forgo you,
I shall give my heart a defence against you,
so that half shall always be armed to abhor you,
though the other half be ready to adore you.

Then, if our love, by loving flourish,
let it not in endless feuding perish;
let us speak no more in jealousy and suspicion.

He offers not part, who would all receive—
so know that when it is your intention
mine shall be to make believe.

JUANA INÉS DE LA CRUZ

litany

Tom, will you let me love you in your restaurant?
i will let you make me a sandwich of your
　　　　invention and i will eat it and call
it a carolyn sandwich. then you will kiss my lips
　　　　and taste the mayonnaise and
that is how you shall love me in my restaurant

Tom, will you come to my empty beige
　　　　apartment and help me set up my daybed?
yes, and i will put the screws in loosely so that
　　　　when we move on it, later,
it will rock like a cradle and then you will know
　　　　you are my baby

Tom, I am sitting on my dirt bike on the deck.
　　　　Will you come out from the kitchen
and watch the people with me?
yes, and then we will race to your bedroom.
　　　　i will win and we will tangle up
on your comforter while the sweat rains from our
　　　　stomachs and foreheads.

Tom, the stars are sitting in tonight like gumball
        gems in a little girl's
jewelry box. Later can we walk to the duck pond?
yes, and we can even go the long way past the
        jungle gym. i will push you on
the swing, but promise me you'll hold tight. if
        you fall i might disappear

Tom, can we make a baby together? I want to be
        a big pregnant woman with a
loved face and give you a squalling red daughter.
no, but i will come inside you and you will be
        my daughter

Tom, will you stay the night with me and sleep
        so close that we are one person?
no, but i will lay down on your sheets and taste
        you. there will be feathers
of you on my tongue and then I will never
        forget you

Tom, when we are in line at the convenience
        store can I put my hands in your

back pockets and my lips and nose in your
        baseball shirt and feel the crook
of your shoulder blade?
no, but later you can lay against me and almost
        touch me and when i go i will
leave my shirt for you to sleep in so that always
        at night you will be pressed
up against the thought of me

Tom, if I weep and want to wait until you need
        me will you promise that someday
you will need me?
no, but i will sit in silence while you rage. you
        can knock the chairs down
any mountain. i will always be the same and you
        will always wait

Tom, will you climb on top of the dumpster and
        steal the sun for me? It's just
hanging there and I want it.
no, it will burn my fingers. no one can have the
        sun: its on loan from god.
but i will draw a picture of it and send it to you
        from richmond and then you

can smooth out the paper and you will have a
        piece of me as well as the sun

Tom, it's so hot here, and I think I'm being
        born. Will you come back from
Richmond and baptise me with sex and cool
        water?
i will come back from richmond. i will smooth
        the damp spiky hairs from the
back of your wet neck and then i will lick the
        salt off it. then i will leave

Tom, Richmond is so far away. How will I know
        how you love me?
i have left you. that is how you will know

CAROLYN CREEDON

Resolve

WHEN YOU'RE DETERMINED TO MOVE ON

You've hit the grit-your-teeth-get-out-of-bed time—no matter how terrible you feel! You've been flooded with feeling for what seems like months now—rage, sadness, self-hatred—but you can no longer be led by these feelings, because they are taking you nowhere. Resolve means that you must ignore your feelings to some extent, put on your cross-trainers, and move one foot in front of the other. (There's a reason that Nike "Just Do It" ad was so popular.) You are finally taking a conscious, deliberate step forward. You may not be entirely sure where you are going and what you might find there, but you understand that anywhere but here is better. There is a certain grimness to this step of recovery. As some of our poets in this section show us, you may have to push and bully your way against the drowning current of pain.

The first inklings of resolve come when you are able to step back from the chaos and pain of your feelings, let go of false hope (which is a killer and keeps you stuck in your misery), and take inventory of your suffering. In her witty, though grim-as-all-get-out "Résumé," Dorothy Parker does exactly that. She totes up the implements of destruction that we have considered literally— yes, we have felt like dying, but razors, guns, gas, and sleeping pills all have their downsides. And figuratively . . . this is our résumé? This is who we are? Who will want us? Who will hire us with such a résumé filled with unhappiness, pain, and disorder? "Right," says Parker, "You might as well live." Resume, then (great pun), begin again. Get off the ledge, listen to the part of yourself that is still intact and begin to see that not every moment is filled with longing, desperation, and pain.

Alice Meynell, in "Renouncement," and Marie Ponsot, in "One Is One," continue the theme of grit and determination. Resolve isn't easy, they tell us; we must actively renounce our tangled emotions and feelings. In fact, the only way to emerge from our wrecked state may be to talk our way out.

Meynell's poem is filled with musts and must nots. She is talking to, advising, admonishing herself: yes, I may need to do this, I should find a mantra and cling to it for a while. "I must not think of thee, the thought of thee must never, never come in sight." She doesn't ask for the impossible—she knows that, like a sentry on guard against feeling, she must eventually sleep and then she will cave. "When night gives pause to the long watch" she keeps, she'll let her guard down, fall asleep, and in her dreams she'll "run, run" to her ex-lover's heart. But when she wakes, she'll be resolute, she tells us; even though "the thought of thee waits hidden yet bright," she'll let go of dreams and "stop short of thee the whole day long."

Ponsot continues the talk-to-yourself therapy. She splits herself in two and rages at her heart: the heart is a bully, a punk, a brute, a spy that has left her shocked and wrecked and still tries to rule the world. Of course we trust our hearts, she says, but sometimes our heart is a double agent that works against us. In a neat twist on the Hank Williams song, Ponsot warns us that it's not his cheating heart, but our own cheating heart that betrays us. To stop the "reel and brawl" of your heart, you must—for a while at least—lock it up, imprison it, become deaf to its rages, and wait for it to think and reform. We love this image of the thinking heart languishing in prison (maybe working in the laundry or making license plates) until it reforms, joins the rest of us, and finally makes us one so that "joy may come." The emphasis here is probably on the may, but Ponsot makes it clear that joy definitely won't come until you get a grip on your heart—and your feelings.

Keep going, writes Derek Walcott in "Winding Up." Keep putting one foot in front of the other, "circle every possibility," and you will wind up somewhere. And for the moment, that place where you wind up may not be as full of joy and sunlight as you imagined when you were wildly in love. Walcott suggests that maybe it's a place of gray water where he can live alone, without wife, children, or love, because love is a stone which has sunk to the bottom of the seabed. Amid the "mediocrity and trash" of the world, there is one thing that makes the speaker in this poem want to live, and that is his own rock-like existence. Steady, watchful, and stripped of emotion, because emotion means encumbrances, he wants to unlearn feelings. Start here, he says, find yourself (your core, your spine), watch the world, strip away the trash, and figure out what you don't want, what you don't need. Realize that "we are what we have made." We have some power and responsibility here, he tells us, we can begin to reconstruct ourselves. And, adds Edgar Bowers in "Amor Vincit Omnia," our very loss and grief will guide us toward this new self. We might begin with "unwilling change," but ultimately, "The mind will change, and change shall be relief."

Elizabeth Bishop, in "One Art," and Louise Glück, in "Lute Song," emphasize both the difficulty and rewards (although the rewards may not be readily apparent in either poem) of resolve. Yes, they say, you've talked yourself out of inertia, you recognize your own responsibility, and now you must act—you must struggle for form, says Glück, and somehow master the disaster of your life. "The art of losing isn't hard to master," says Bishop. In fact, we lose something every day— we learn to accept the loss of small things, door keys, names, and houses that we have loved. And after we have practiced loss, "losing farther and faster," we can even accept the loss of the beloved. Here the speaker breaks down for a moment: "the joking voice, a gesture I love." She makes the loss real for us. We must, she says, face it, say it, "*Write* it!" The *write it* works another way here—make it right again, so that we can master not just the art of losing, but go forward and begin to master the art of living.

Résumé

Razors pain you;
Rivers are damp;
Acids stain you;
And drugs cause cramp.
Guns aren't lawful;
Nooses give;
Gas smells awful;
You might as well live.

DOROTHY PARKER

Renouncement

I must not think of thee; and, tired yet strong,
I shun the thought that lurks in all delight—
    The thought of thee—and in the blue
        heaven's height,
And in the sweetest passage of a song.
Oh, just beyond the fairest thoughts that throng
    This breast, the thought of thee waits hidden
        yet bright;
But it must never, never come in sight;
I must stop short of thee the whole day long.
But when sleep comes to close each difficult day,
    When night gives pause to the long watch I
        keep,
And all my bonds I needs must loose apart,
Must doff my will as raiment laid away,—
    With the first dream that comes with the first
        sleep
I run, I run, I am gathered to thy heart.

ALICE MEYNELL

One Is One

Heart, you bully, you punk, I'm wrecked,
     I'm shocked
stiff. You? You still try to rule the world—though
I've got you: identified, starving, locked
in a cage you will not leave alive, no
matter how you hate it, pound its walls
& thrill its corridors with messages.

Brute. Spy. I trusted you. Now you reel & brawl
in your cell but I'm deaf to your rages,
your greed to go solo, your eloquent
threats of worse things you (knowing me)
     could do.
You scare me, bragging you're a double agent

since jailers are prisoners' prisoners too.
Think! Reform! Make us one. Join the rest of us,
and joy may come, and make its test of us.

MARIE PONSOT

Winding Up

I live on the water,
alone. Without wife and children.
I have circled every possibility
to come to this:

a low house by grey water,
with windows always open
to the stale sea. We do not choose such things,

but we are what we have made.
We suffer, the years pass,
we shed freight but not our need

for encumbrances. Love is a stone
that settled on the sea-bed
under grey water. Now I require nothing

from poetry but true feeling,
no pity, no fame, no healing. Silent wife,
we can sit watching grey water,

and in a life awash
with mediocrity and trash
live rock-like.

I shall unlearn feeling,
unlearn my gift. That is greater
and harder than what passes there for life.

DEREK WALCOTT

Amor Vincit Omnia

Love is no more.
It died as the mind dies: the pure desire
Relinquishing the blissful form it wore,
The ample joy and clarity expire.

Regret is vain.
Then do not grieve for what you would efface,
The sudden failure of the past, the pain
Of its unwilling change, and the disgrace.

Leave innocence,
And modify your nature by the grief
Which poses to the will indifference
That no desire is permanent in sense.

Take leave of me.
What recompense, or pity, or deceit
Can cure, or what assumed serenity
Conceal the mortal loss which we repeat?

The mind will change, and change shall be relief.

EDGAR BOWERS

One Art

The art of losing isn't hard to master;
so many things seem filled with intent
to be lost that their loss is no disaster.

Lose something every day. Accept the fluster
of lost door keys, the hour badly spent.
The art of losing isn't hard to master.

Then practice losing farther, losing faster:
places, and names, and where it was you meant
to travel. None of these will bring disaster.

I lost my mother's watch. And look! my last, or
next-to-last, of three loved houses went.
The art of losing isn't hard to master.

I lost two cities, lovely ones. And, vaster,
some realms I owned, two rivers, a continent.
I miss them, but it wasn't a disaster.

—Even losing you (the joking voice, a gesture
I love) I shan't have lied. It's evident
the art of losing's not too hard to master
though it may look like (*Write* it!) like disaster.

ELIZABETH BISHOP

Lute Song

No one wants to be the muse;
in the end, everyone wants to be Orpheus.

Valiantly reconstructed
(out of terror and pain)
and then overwhelmingly beautiful;

restoring, ultimately,
not Eurydice, the lamented one,
but the ardent
spirit of Orpheus, made present

not as a human being, rather
as pure soul rendered
detached, immortal,
through deflected narcissism.

I made a harp of disaster
to perpetuate the beauty of my last love.
Yet my anguish, such as it is,
remains the struggle for form

and my dreams, if I speak openly,
less the wish to be remembered
than the wish to survive,
which is, I believe, the deepest human wish.

LOUISE GLÜCK

Relapse
WHEN YOU'D GIVE
ANYTHING TO GO BACK

This time, you're really over it. (Or so you've told yourself.) No calling, no e-mailing, no talking to your friends about him. You're going to shake it off, get a grip, tough it out. Sure, it *sounds* good, but that kind of grim determination leaves you exhausted. All you want to do is relax back into something easy and familiar. You want the past back . . . no, you want *him* back. . . . Safely locked in the golden past of your memory, he shimmers with perfection.

No doubt about it, you're in major Relapse. But who can blame you, really? You're fighting an addiction to love, to pain, and to the idealized past. At the mercy of your cravings, you think, just one more call, one more e-mail, just one more night or day or afternoon of him. He calls, he comes over, he spends the night, but nothing has changed. He still wants out, and you're freshly crushed. Again. And even if you've kept yourself from actual physical relapses, in your head you're constantly replaying the movie of your relationship. You want it all back, every shining, perfect moment. (Conveniently, you don't remember the bad stuff, the way he sometimes dumped you at parties and flirted with other women, the time he borrowed eight hundred dollars to get his car fixed and never paid it back because "Remember, I spent a bundle on that trip to the beach for your birthday.") You know it's self-destructive, you know it keeps you suspended in time and pain and despair, but you can't help yourself.

Don't think you're a hopeless case. Relapses, experts tell us, are normal and necessary. Cold turkey almost never works. No one gets through the recovery process without relapsing. The intervals between relapses get longer and longer until you finally recover completely. In the meantime, we think that these poems can help us forgive ourselves for our relapses. They show us that sometimes we are powerless against our heart's desires, that our idealized notions of "true love" are deeply embedded in our battered hearts, but ultimately we don't need to throw out the past. It will stay with us in a way that enriches rather than diminishes us.

To fully appreciate the first Relapse poem, you must come to it with an open mind and a lot of empathy for young women who make mistakes in love (the way we all do). This is actual testimony from the grand jury investigation into the Bill Clinton-Monica Lewinsky relationship, arranged into a poem by poet Tom Simon. Here we have Monica before the jury, forced to answer questions about her relationship with the president. She tries to say as little as possible, to keep her words matter-of-fact: "We would talk about our childhoods/Talk about current events." But she can't quite pull it off when she testifies, "When I was with him/It was a lot of—" And we think, what was it a lot of, Monica? Lies? Deceit? Bullshit? But no, she loses herself in the past, in her memories of Bill, and concludes dreamily, "He was sunshine." And we see it, we understand—no matter what we think of Monica Lewinsky, we know that feeling.

And so does the speaker in Robert Frost's "A Late Walk." He, too, is filled with resolve. The hour is late, the day is bare and brown, and he's going to take a walk by himself, to work through the sadness he feels. But he doesn't go far before he finds himself "picking the faded blue/Of the last remaining aster flower," which he will carry again to the person he loves. Sometimes we just can't keep ourselves from old habits and desires, from wanting only what's worn, known, and familiar.

Of course there's comfort in what we're used to. There's security and order in routine, no surprises. The speaker in Norma Tilden's "The New Dog" used to sit on the stairs with her old dog each morning, trying to hold him still as she put on her shoes. He was part of the family, featured in "the center of all our pictures," even getting a birthday countdown and cake. Now he's gone, and there's a new dog who "pushes into the space you left/in the airy curve of my arm/where it circled your belly." In Relapse, our very bodies become reminders of what we've lost; we ache to have the past back in our arms. But Tilden's poem reminds us that these relapses are momentary. There's a new dog clamoring for attention in the here and now, and even though he's fat and "breathes too loud," she's going to give him the affection he wants.

So there *is* hope. Having someone new to love certainly increases your chances of moving beyond Relapse, but only if your heart is in it. What usually happens in Relapse is you let yourself start dating again, but some part of you stubbornly insists that no one will ever know you as well as he did. You convince yourself that nothing can come close to the pure bond you two once shared. You'll go out on a date here and there, but you'll always find something wrong with the guy (hairy back, buck teeth, chews with his mouth open, too nice, too dumb, likes Christina Aguilera, hates Macy Gray). Why go through all the bother of dealing with them when you can sink back into glorious memories of what you think you once had?

Why do we do this to ourselves, cling to some impossible picture of love? Why do we rewrite the history of our own relationship, making it into some *Romeo and Juliet* tragedy, when in fact we know we were anxious and unhappy a lot of the time? For one thing, we're lonely. Suddenly there's this big hole in our days, this silence and extra empty time. So we fill it by telling ourselves this beautiful story of lost love; it's the curse of "True Love." Like the speaker in Wislawa Szymborska's poem, we believe such a thing actually exists. For some reason, we buy into the whole idealized notion of fairytale love, the big-time Cinderella-gets-her-prince-and-Christopher Plummer-dumps-the-countess-for-a-perky-nun and-Richard-Gere-the-magnate-rescues-Julia Roberts-the-prostitute kind of love, all set to the sound of heart-wrenching music. Oh, the bliss of it all!

No matter how cynical we may want to be (to protect ourselves from disappointment), of course we want to believe in True Love, too. But we think that in order to get past Relapse, you need to start seeing the difference between the real and the ideal. Mythical True Love offers drama and titillation, beauty and nobility, all the things our Relapse poets dwell on. Of course we want it all! We want the sizzling chemistry John Donne

RELAPSE

describes in "The Flea." The speaker in the poem flirts with his lover in a sexy, clever way, claiming that he and she are bound together by the blood in the flea which has bitten them both. "This flea is you and I, and this/Our marriage bed, and marriage temple is," he tells his bemused lover. We swoon for guys like this who know how to tease and seduce—but is this love?

No one has a bad hair day or a blemish in True Love. Everyone is laughing and beautiful like the speaker in Maturai Eruttalan Centamputan's "What She Said." Her "arms had the grace of the bamboo" and her "forehead was mistaken for the moon" when her True Lover loved her. In other words, the power of his love made her beautiful, special, magical. But was she really loved or just admired? The end of the poem reads simply "But now." But now, it seems, the magic is gone, the slipper didn't fit after all. She's ordinary again, beyond the glow of True Love. The speaker in Georgia Douglas Johnson's "I Want To Die While You Love Me" can't bear the thought of living that way; she'd rather die than lose the glory and perfection True Love brings to her life. Is love supposed to make everything perfect? What about those days when you're not "fair" (bad bloat), and no "laughter lies upon [your] lips" (big cold sore), and you've got no "lights in [your] hair" (bedhead)—True Love may desert you, but will real true love still smile on you then?

Once you sort out the real from the ideal, you can remember your old relationship with new clarity. We don't have to reject the past in order to live in the present, say Edwin Morgan and Billy Collins. As long as we're honest with ourselves, the past will always stay with us in a valuable way. So replay the picture-perfect moments, as the speaker does in Morgan's "Strawberries": "There were never strawberries/like the ones we had/that sultry afternoon." Feel that pang of loss, crave one more taste of *those* strawberries, and be glad that once you did experience that magic. It's part of who you are now, and you're richer for it. Like the speaker in Collins's "This Much I Do Remember," you're allowed to rescue special moments, to carry them in the "pocket" of your memory, and to realize that they are "minted in the kingdom/that we pace through every day." In other words, every day the world is coining new treasures for us; every minute holds the promise of new memories, new hope, new love.

So you have a choice: stay in Relapse and impoverish your heart, or move on to Real Hope and strike it rich in the kingdom of the present.

Sunshine

We would tell jokes
We would talk about our childhoods
Talk about current events

I was always giving him
My stupid ideas
About what I thought should be done
In the administration or
Different views on things

I think back on it
And he always made me smile
When I was with him

It was a lot of—
He was sunshine

TOM SIMON, ED.

A Late Walk

When I go up through the mowing field,
The headless aftermath,
Smooth-laid like thatch with the heavy dew,
Half closes the garden path.

And when I come to the garden ground,
The whir of sober birds
Up from the tangle of withered weeds
Is sadder than any words.

A tree beside the wall stands bare,
But a leaf that lingered brown,
Disturbed, I doubt not, by my thought,
Comes softly rattling down.

I end not far from my going forth,
By picking the faded blue
Of the last remaining aster flower
To carry again to you.

ROBERT FROST

The New Dog

Already fat, now pushes into the space you left
in the airy curve of my arm
where it circled your belly
as I tried to hold you still
each morning, sitting on the stairs, putting on
my outside shoes

Has the same coarse black hair, knots and cords,
the same wooly smell.

Shapeless with fur, he photographs badly
as you did—
an inky blot in the center of all our pictures,
easily mistaken for a garbage bag
with a pink, flapping tie.

"He breathes too loud"—
my father's last words
on the new dog, wild with wanting things, even
     the air.

But tonight, with his birthday two days off,
I found the note you made me post in the kitchen
year after year,
the spelling so bad that we knew
these words had come from you—
a dog's transcription of the gruff commands
you heard us give each other,
tossing voices back and forth like balls:

   "Elefin" . . . written, then crossed out,
   "Fif" . . . crossed out again, then
   "Wun
   Mo Das
   Til Mi Birthda.
   I WANT CAK!"

Too rough for words,
this new dog
may never write me letters.
But he, too, wants cake.
And now that you remind me
I will probably make one for him.

NORMA TILDEN

True Love

True love. Is it normal,
is it serious, is it practical?
What does the world get from two people
who exist in a world of their own?

Placed on the same pedestal for no good reason,
drawn randomly from millions, but convinced
it had to happen this way—in reward for what?
    For nothing.
The light descends from nowhere.
Why on these two and not on others?
Doesn't this outrage justice? Yes it does.
Doesn't it disrupt our painstakingly erected
        principles,
and cast the moral from the peak? Yes on both
        accounts.

Look at the happy couple.
Couldn't they at least try to hide it,
fake a little depression for their friends' sake!
Listen to them laughing—it's an insult.
The language they use—deceptively clear.

And their little celebrations, rituals,
the elaborate mutual routines—
it's obviously a plot behind the human race's back!

It's hard even to guess how far things might go
if people start to follow their example.
What could religion and poetry count on?
What would be remembered? What renounced?
Who'd want to stay within bounds?

True love. Is it really necessary?
Tact and common sense tell us to pass over it in
        silence,
like a scandal in Life's highest circles.
Perfectly good children are born without its help.
It couldn't populate the planet in a million years,
it comes along so rarely.

Let the people who never find true love
keep saying that there's no such thing.

Their faith will make it easier for them to live
        and die.

WISLAWA SZYMBORSKA

The Flea

Marke but this flea, and marke in this,
How little that which thou deny'st me is;
It suck'd me first, and now sucks thee,
And in this flea, our two bloods mingled bee;
Thou know'st that this cannot be said
A sinne, nor shame, nor loss of maidenhead,
    Yet this enjoyes before it wooe,
    And pamper'd swells with one blood made of
        two
    And this, alas, is more then wee would doe.

Oh stay, three lives in one flea spare,
Where wee almost, yea more then maryed are.
This flea is you and I, and this
Our mariage bed, and mariage temple is;
Though parents grudge, and you, w'are met,
And cloystered in these living walls of Jet.
    Though use make you apt to kill mee,
    Let not to that, selfe murder added bee,
    And sacrilege, three sinnes in killing three.

Cruell and sodaine, hast thou since
Purpled thy naile, in blood of innocence?
Wherein could this flea guilty bee,
Except in that drop which it suckt from thee?
Yet thou triumph'st, and saist that thou
Find'st not thy selfe, nor mee the weaker now;
  'Tis true, then learne how false, feares bee;
  Just so much honor, when thou yeeld'st to mee,
  Will wast, as this flea's death tooke life from thee.

JOHN DONNE

What She Said

Before I laughed with him
    nightly,

     the slow waves beating
     on his wide shores
     and the palmyra
     bringing forth heron-like flowers
     near the waters,

my eyes were like the lotus
my arms had the grace of the bamboo
my forehead was mistaken for the moon.

    But now.

MATURAI ERUTTALAN CENTAMPUTAN

I Want to Die While You Love Me

I want to die while you love me,
While yet you hold me fair,
While laughter lies upon my lips
And lights are in my hair.

I want to die while you love me,
And bear to that still bed
Your kisses turbulent, unspent,
To warm me when I'm dead.

I want to die while you love me
Oh, who would care to live
Till love has nothing more to ask
And nothing more to give!

I want to die while you love me
And never, never see
The glory of this perfect day
Grow dim or cease to be.

GEORGIA DOUGLAS JOHNSON

Strawberries

There were never strawberries
like the ones we had
that sultry afternoon
sitting on the step
of the open french window
facing each other
your knees held in mine
the blue plates in our laps
the strawberries glistening
in the hot sunlight
we dipped them in sugar
looking at each other
not hurrying the feast
for one to come
the empty plates
laid on the stone together
with the two forks crossed
and I bent towards you
sweet in that air
in my arms
abandoned like a child
from your eager mouth

the taste of strawberries
in my memory
lean back again
let me love you
let the sun beat
on our forgetfulness
one hour of all
the heat intense
and summer lightning
on the Kilpatrick hills

let the storm wash the plates.

EDWIN MORGAN

This Much I Do Remember

It was after dinner.
You were talking to me across the table
about something or other,
a greyhound you had seen that day
or a song you liked,

and I was looking past you
over your bare shoulder
at the three oranges lying
on the kitchen counter
next to the small electric bean grinder,
which was also orange,
and the orange and white cruets for vinegar
        and oil.

All of which converged
into a random still life,
so fastened together by the hasp of color,
and so fixed behind the animated
foreground of your
talking and smiling,
gesturing and pouring wine,
and the camber of your shoulders

that I could feel it being painted within me,
brushed on the wall of my skull,
while the tone of your voice
lifted and fell in its flight,
and the three oranges
remained fixed on the counter
the way stars are said
to be fixed in the universe.

Then all the moments of the past
began to line up behind that moment
and all the moments to come
assembled in front of it in a long row,
giving me reason to believe
that this was a moment I had rescued

from the millions that rush out of sight
into a darkness behind the eyes.

Even after I have forgotten what year it is,
my middle name,
and the meaning of money,
I will still carry in my pocket
the small coin of that moment,
minted in the kingdom
that we pace through every day.

BILLY COLLINS

Real Hope

WHEN YOU REDISCOVER
YOURSELF AND YOUR
STRENGTHS

At last! Real hope! Finally you've come to terms with the fact that you're not repulsive, irredeemably screwed up, or destined never to be with anyone again (self-hatred). You don't want to fake that you're better (false hope), force yourself to feel better (resolve), or fantasize that having him back will make you feel better (relapse). You want you back, the you that existed happily before you ever knew him, the you that you lost somewhere along the way.

That's why we love Real Hope. Finally, after all the breakup hell, someone gets to get back together—and it's you! With yourself!

Sure, maybe it sounds self-absorbed, this self-love, but that's not what we mean. We mean you're joyful again. We mean you're taking care of yourself again—working out, eating full meals, keeping your place clean and pretty—not because you want to snag someone new, but because you want to feel healthy and whole and happy.

The poems in this section are all about the liberation that real hope brings. Lighten yourself, the Chippewa poem tells us. Drop the burden of self-pity, because you are "being carried on great winds across the sky." Something larger than we know holds us in its arms "all the time," even when we feel most alone, and moves us forward in life. Whether you believe in some benevolent force or not, you can still take comfort in the notion that you are connected to a world that is grand, sweeping, and full of possibility every day. You're allowed to have faith in that world, to trust it again.

Not that it's the least bit easy to maintain this kind of faith. It takes patience and practice. That's the "reality" part of "real hope." You realize that only you can give yourself the kind of emotional shelter and sustenance you need. So, like the speaker in William Butler Yeats's "The Lake Isle of Innisfree," you decide to "arise and go now," to build your small cabin of clay, plant your tidy bean-rows, and tend your hive. You decide to spend time and effort on the things you enjoy, the things you're good at.

While that may seem like a simple, practical decision—you have to get on with your life, after all—we think it takes a heroic amount of hope, because it means accepting that you're going to "live alone" and like it. There's no Tom Cruise/Jerry Maguire around to "complete you," no Prince Charming to help you plant those bean-rows happily ever after. It's tough to pretend you don't feel the stigma of being single in a society that seems to celebrate coupledom. All around you the "marrieds" have their family-full lives and constant companionship, their fabulous wedding present dishes and gadgets—and there you are, in full Ally McBeal–ish spinster splendor. How are you, post-breakup, all by yourself, without double incomes or SUV-sized baby strollers, or even just an automatic date for weddings, supposed to find any peace or joy in your "small cabin" all alone?

Yeats might answer that there's beauty in solitude and peace in the satisfaction of a simple life well lived. Quietly tend your bee hive (nurture your talents, reach out to others), and soon you find yourself living in a bee-loud glade, where "midnight's all a glimmer, and noon a purple glow,/And evening full of the linnet wings." Your world looks good to you again; you're centered and happy, filling your place with fresh flowers, and having friends over for dinner the way you used to. Before you know it, "peace comes dropping slow" around you, like the murmur of "lake water lapping with low sounds by the shore." In your "deep heart's core" you know you're ready to live fully again.

Living fully doesn't necessarily mean that you cram your day full of activity or go climb Everest or become the next Mother Teresa. It could just mean taking pleasure in who you are at this moment, making full use of all of your senses. Just breathe. Stretch. Notice beauty and laughter. Feed yourself—figuratively and literally—because you're hungry for life again and because, well, who doesn't love to eat? Follow the "get over a breakup" recipe Jane Hirshfield gives in her poem "Da Capo." First, toss out your "used-up heart like a pebble," and then once you're back home, slice and glaze vegetables and herbs, throw in a little spice and cheese (and parsley for color), and "Eat." Nourishing yourself (body and soul) is the best way to "begin again the story of your life."

Or try more of a Willy Wonka approach, like the speaker in Kate Bingham's "Home Sweet Home." Who needs a boyfriend when you can live in a "chocolate bar" house? Imagine a home made of cocoa and nougat, with butterscotch hallways, wafer walls, and rooms sweet as icing sugar. Like the cabin in Innisfree, this home offers nothing too fancy, but it does provide the peace of mind that comes from knowing "There's only me, I know exactly what I'm looking for." In Real Hope you know your own mind and tastes again, and you revel in that knowledge. No wonder the speaker can't wait to come home, "drop [her] hand-bag in the hall,/tie back [her] hair, lie down and lick the floor."

But it's not all sweetness and light in Real Hope—you're almost to the Moving On stage, but not quite there. You're happy again but still have moments of doubt and maybe even twinges of pain. Don't think that means you're sliding back to hell—it just means you're normal. You've lost someone, and the hurt from that doesn't ever completely go away. Plus, your judgment's been shaken, so you're not completely sure you can trust your perceptions and feelings. Everyone tells you that you're back to your old self, but like the speaker in A. E. Housman's "O When I Was in Love with You," you wonder if it's true. You worry that you're tainted or damaged; you suspect you're not nearly as confident and carefree as you once were. Maybe you even fear that love itself isn't the "clean and brave" thing you once believed in.

Real Hope is all about confronting those doubts: am I really feeling better? am I really over this? does the whole world suck or am I allowed to be happy again? And then being able to answer, I AM BETTER, AND THE WORLD DOESN'T SUCK! There's true victory in real hope, when you know you've stared down the rage and sadness and pain and emerged fuller, stronger, and maybe even happier than you were before.

The speaker in Jane Kenyon's "In the Grove: The Poet at Ten," for example, is feeling tired and sad, when she notices a cloud passing over the sun. Even though the cloud is huge, it can't completely block the sun. When "the light surge[s] back again," the speaker experiences a "joy so violent it was hard to distinguish from pain." That's the kind of joy you want to feel at this stage, the kind that reminds you that you *have* triumphed over "violent pain," that the best part of you *can* surge back. Louise Glück's speaker in "Vespers" feels that same kind of victorious glee when she declares that she alone is responsible for her tomato plants. No matter what God and the elements throw at her (heavy rains, cold nights, the blight that breaks her heart), she's going to make her garden grow.

In Real Hope, you're able to acknowledge that happiness is possible despite the blight and cold nights of heartbreak. In fact we would argue (along with poets Robert Frost and Yevgeny Yevtushenko) that happiness is *only* possible because of things like pain. The speaker in Frost's "To Earthward" used to crave the intense sweetness of infatuation, when the mere touching of lips is too much to bear, when you live on air charged with the "swirl and ache/From sprays of honeysuckle." But he's learned that cotton-candy love like that can't sustain him through life. Now he craves a rough, real, earthly love, the kind that can carry him through the "weariness and fault" of daily existence, the kind that acknowledges there is "no joy . . . that is not dashed with pain." And the only way to get that real human love, Yevtushenko tells us in "Lies," is to face a few human facts—"sorrow happens, hardship happens"—and then to say "The hell with it." Because it's only by accepting those truths that we can truly understand what it means to be happy. Or as the speaker says, "Who never knew the price of happiness will not be happy."

So the hell with heartbreak. You're you again, and ready to move on.

Sometimes I Go About Pitying Myself

Sometimes I go about pitying myself,
and all the time
I am being carried on great winds across the sky.

CHIPPEWA MUSIC
adapted from the translation
by Frances Densmore

The Lake Isle of Innisfree

I will arise and go now, and go to Innisfree,
And a small cabin build there, of clay and
      wattles made:
Nine bean-rows will I have there, a hive for the
      honey-bee,
And live alone in the bee-loud glade.

And I shall have some peace there, for peace
      comes dropping slow,
Dropping from the veils of the morning to
      where the cricket sings;
There midnight's all a-glimmer, and noon a
      purple glow,
And evening full of the linnet's wings.

I will arise and go now, for always night and day
I hear lake water lapping with low sounds by the
      shore;
While I stand on the roadway, or on the
      pavements grey,
I hear it in the deep heart's core.

WILLIAM BUTLER YEATS

Da Capo

Take the used-up heart like a pebble
and throw it far out.

Soon there is nothing left.
Soon the last ripple exhausts itself
in the weeds.

Returning home, slice carrots, onions, celery.
Glaze them in oil before adding
the lentils, water, and herbs.

Then the roasted chestnuts, a little pepper,
        the salt.
Finish with goat cheese and parsley. Eat.

You may do this, I tell you, it is permitted.
Begin again the story of your life.

JANE HIRSHFIELD

Home Sweet Home

I need a chocolate bar I can live with,
nothing too big, a red-brick biscuit base, perhaps,
south-facing, on a quiet, tree-lined residential
     street
where parking late at night won't be a problem.

Nothing too crumbly either. I don't want
to be sweeping up bits of cornice all weekend
and pestering the surveyor with each new crack
in the milky bar matt emulsion shell.

It's got to be the sort of place I can forget about,
with cocoa solids minimum 65 per cent
and nougat foundations limed with soya lecithin
cement and bourneville guttering

no matter what the cost because you can't price
peace of mind and that means no original features,
nothing too fancy, nothing architect-designed.
There's only me, I know exactly what I'm
          looking for,

not space so much as surface area, a
          honey-comb interior,
with wafer walls and butterscotch parquet
leading from room to room, each mouthful lighter,
sweeter than the one before and breathed, not
          tasted,

like a puff of icing sugar. Coming home
will be a hit, a score. I'll drop my hand-bag in
          the hall,
tie back my hair, lie down and lick the floor.

KATE BINGHAM

Oh, When I Was in Love with You

Oh, when I was in love with you,
   Then I was clean and brave,
And miles around the wonder grew
   How well did I behave.

And now the fancy passes by,
   And nothing will remain,
And miles around they'll say that I
   Am quite myself again.

A. E. HOUSMAN

In the Grove: The Poet at Ten

She lay on her back in the timothy
and gazed past the doddering
auburn heads of sumac.

A cloud—huge, calm,
and dignified—covered the sun
but did not, could not, put it out.

The light surged back again.

Nothing could rouse her then
from that joy so violent
it was hard to distinguish from pain.

JANE KENYON

The Pruned Tree

As a torn paper might seal up its side,
Or a streak of water stitch itself to silk
And disappear, my wound has been my healing,
And I am made more beautiful by losses.
See the flat water in the distance nodding
Approval, the light that fell in love with statues,
Seeing me alive, turn its motion toward me.
Shorn, I rejoice in what was taken from me.

What can the moonlight do with my new shape
But trace and retrace its miracle of order?
I stand, waiting for the strange reaction
Of insects who knew me in my larger self,
Unkempt, in a naturalness I did not love.
Even the dog's voice rings with a new echo,
And all the little leaves I shed are singing,
Singing to the moon of shapely newness.

Somewhere what I lost I hope is springing
To life again. The roofs, astonished by me,
Are taking new bearings in the night, the owl
Is crying for a further wisdom, the lilac
Putting forth its strongest scent to find me.
Butterflies, like sails in grooves, are winging
Out of the water to wash me, wash me.
Now, I am stirring like a seed in China.

HOWARD MOSS

Vespers

In your extended absence, you permit me
use of earth, anticipating
some return on investment. I must report
failure in my assignment, principally
regarding the tomato plants.
I think I should not be encouraged to grow
tomatoes. Or, if I am, you should withhold
the heavy rains, the cold nights that come
so often here, while other regions get
twelve weeks of summer. All this
belongs to you: on the other hand,
I planted the seeds, I watched the first shoots
like wings tearing the soil, and it was my heart
broken by the blight, the black spot so quickly
multiplying in the rows. I doubt
you have a heart, in our understanding of
that term. You who do not discriminate
between the dead and the living, who are, in
        consequence,

immune to foreshadowing, you may not know
how much terror we bear, the spotted leaf,
the red leaves of the maple falling
even in August, in early darkness: I am responsible
for these vines.

LOUISE GLÜCK

To Earthward

Love at the lips was touch
As sweet as I could bear;
And once that seemed too much;
I lived on air

That crossed me from sweet things,
The flow of—was it musk
From hidden grapevine springs
Downhill at dusk?

I had the swirl and ache
From sprays of honeysuckle
That when they're gathered shake
Dew on the knuckle.

I craved strong sweets, but those
Seemed strong when I was young;
The petal of the rose
It was that stung.

Now no joy but lacks salt,
That is not dashed with pain
And weariness and fault;
I crave the stain

Of tears, the aftermark
Of almost too much love,
The sweet of bitter bark
And burning clove.

When stiff and sore and scarred
I take away my hand
From leaning on it hard
In grass and sand,

The hurt is not enough:
I long for weight and strength
To feel the earth as rough
To all my length.

ROBERT FROST

Lies

Lying to the young is wrong.
Proving to them that lies are true is wrong.
Telling them
                that God's in his heaven
and all's well with the world
                        is wrong.
They know what you mean.
                    They are people too.
Tell them the difficulties
                  can't be counted,
and let them see
            not only
                what will be
but see
      with clarity
            these present times.
Say obstacles exist they must encounter,
sorrow comes,
           hardship happens.
The hell with it.
           Who never knew
the price of happiness
             will not be happy.

Forgive no error
                    you recognize,
it will repeat itself,
                    a hundredfold
and afterward
                    our pupils
will not forgive in us
                    what we forgave.

YEVGENY YEVTUSHENKO

Moving On

WHEN YOU REDISCOVER THE WORLD AND ITS JOYS

The miraculous thing about the Moving On stage is that it just kind of happens when you're not paying attention. One day you're out doing your usual thing and someone asks how you are, and you find yourself answering automatically, "Great! Everything's really great!" It almost catches you by surprise to hear yourself happy. Back in the "I hate myself and the world" days you wanted to rip the face off of anyone who dared ask you that question, and then you'd grit your teeth through some fake-perky response. Now the smile comes easily and so does the answer: you're just fine.

Moving On is our favorite stage (though Rage has a certain vengeful charm). Finally the world and all its joys matter to you again. You're having fun and making plans, even dating again. Your life revolves around your interests and goals, not around him or e-mails you hope might come from him or photographs and memories of him. It's a time of growth and celebration, so we stuffed this section like a piñata, full of "the world is wonderful" poems. Some make you laugh, others offer comfort, and all help remind you that you have a place and purpose in this world. You can come back to these poems again and again, because ultimately they're not just about how to move on from a romantic breakup, they're about how to live with grace, humor, and courage, no matter what losses you may encounter. And you *will* encounter them if you're going to live fully in the world.

So how do you make sure you keep Moving On through love and life? The poets in this section have a range of answers, and we've grouped the poems according to the advice they offer.

First, try acceptance. Accept that loss is part of life, and that sometimes loss leads to fulfillment. This doesn't mean that you passively just let things slip away from you, that you pretend not to care. It means being brave enough to grab what you can while you can, even though you

know it may not last (think Kate and Leonardo in
Titanic, or Humphrey and Ingrid in *Casablanca*).
"In Blackwater Woods," Mary Oliver tells it to us
straight:

> *To live in this world*
>
> *you must be able*
> *to do three things:*
> *to love what is mortal;*
> *to hold it*
>
> *against your bones knowing*
> *your own life depends on it;*
> *and, when the time comes to let it go,*
> *to let it go.*

Letting go of something doesn't necessarily
mean you lose that something. Look at the
speaker in Elizabeth Bishop's "The Fish," for
example. She catches a tremendous fish, but
instead of hauling it in just for the sake of it, she
allows herself to feel something for him, to
admire his dignity and the way he's survived cap-

ture five times. By releasing him, she loses him, but wins redemption for herself. Her crummy rented boat, with its "rusted engine" fills up with victory and all she can see is "rainbow, rainbow, rainbow." She is transformed because she has the heart to let go.

Acceptance means acknowledging the rhythm of ebb and flow, night and day, sorrow and happiness. Jane Kenyon's "Let Evening Come" shows us there's beauty and peace in the "light of late afternoon," while Billy Collins's "Morning" offers us the A.M. joy of "buzzing around the house on espresso." The point is we can't fight either one—night will come as surely as morning, and joy as surely as mourning—so we might as well try to find solace in both.

Life may have certain inevitabilities; we all suffer in our "doggy" lives, says W. H. Auden, and the world still goes on its merry way, oblivious. But that doesn't mean you have to roll over and let the universe just have its way with you. Don't wait for the world to give you what it can; like Peter in Mark Doty's "Tiara," you need to "ask for it." Go ahead; you're allowed. You've earned the right to be here in Moving On. After all of that suffering and doubt and praying and trying, you have arrived in the Promised Land of Over It. Like the speaker in Kim Konopka's "Upon Entering," announce your presence with defiance. "Kick open the saloon doors" of this new place and lasso yourself a life of joy and celebration.

Get out in the world and revel in all it has to offer. "O taste and see," urges the speaker in Denise Levertov's poem of the same name. Pluck the fruit in the orchard, and then "savor, chew, swallow, transform." In other words, test your talents, pursue your passions, and let those experiences lead you to a sure sense of who you are. Build a strong core for yourself so that almost nothing and no one can shake you from that foundation. Think Madonna: always experimenting with her look, her sound, her men (pre-Guy), but always very definitely Madonna. You may not like her, but you can't say she doesn't know how to move on.

Don't be afraid to know what you want and to go after it. The speaker in May Swenson's "Strawberrying," for example, turns strawberry picking into a fierce, sensual conquest. Her hands are "murder-red" with the juice of the berries she's ravished from a crop that "begs for plunder." And not just any berries will do—she only wants the "sweet hearts young and firm," the plump ones with perfect flesh and soft nippled heads. Nothing too soft—she leaves those to rot in the heat—and certainly not the "spiderspit-gray" ones that are "still attached to their dead stems." Let your friends call you picky, but know that you're allowed to be discriminating in your choice of a man or anything else you want in your life. If you settle for less, you're as intact but empty as the berries hidden under moldy leaves.

If this all sounds a bit too I-am-bitch-hear-me-roar-ish, well, we only mean to encourage you to go after what you want in a deliberate, mindful way. We've seen too many friends throw themselves back into the world like spinning tops in a Skittles game, whirling all over creation, taking pilates/swing dance/kick-boxing, joining three book clubs, seeing two therapists, attempting one blind date a week—and winding up exhausted. There are loads of wonderful things to do and learn when you're moving on, but as the speaker in Robert Morgan's "Honey" advises: Resist greed. If you want to get the honey out of the hive without being stung, that is, if you want a life of fulfillment, not frustration: maintain calmness, and approach with confidence.

One of the best ways to attain that kind of calm confidence, we think, is to lighten up. Laugh a little! Stop taking everyone so seriously, including yourself. Remember that Brady Bunch episode where the only way Marcia can pass her driving test is to envision the test-giver in his underwear? Weird episode. But the point is to hone a healthy sense of irreverence. Recognize that we all are really only human with our own frailties and comical-looking genitalia (see "Teste Moanial," by Anne McNaughton). We're all goofy and messed-up in our own spectacular ways, so don't let yourself judge people too harshly, even your ex or your ex's new girlfriend. It makes you mean and bitter and ugly, and you'll never move on that way. Develop your senses of humor and compassion instead.

While you're at it, try giving something back

to the world. Remember back in the Sadness and Self-Hatred days when you just couldn't find a reason to get up in the morning? When you felt there was nothing you could do that was worth anything? In Moving On you "shake off that sluggish[ness]" and decide to "throw yourself like seed as you walk" (Miguel De Unamuno, "Throw Yourself Like Seed"). You have a purpose in life, and a responsibility to fulfill that purpose—you want your seed to take root. So find your vocation, and take pleasure in doing your work well. In Billy Collins's "Picnic, Lightning," the speaker is merely shoveling compost, but still he takes time to notice the marvels in the soil and the wild blue color of the wheelbarrow. And in Robert Frost's "Mowing," the speaker is only cutting the grass, but he goes about his work with earnest love. He doesn't want easy gold (like the lottery) or idle hours (like what you might have when you win the lottery), he wants the satisfaction of being good at what he does.

That's what moving on is ultimately about, that feeling of fulfillment and capability. Life *will* break your heart, but you have the ability to mend it. You have the ability to live deliberately and joyfully. You're alive and kicking in this "gay great happening illimitably earth," so like the speaker in e.e. cummings's "i thank You God for most this amazing," be grateful for what you've got. Think George Bailey in the last part of *It's a Wonderful Life*, laughing and crying because his cut is bleeding again and he's found Zuzu's petals in his pocket. Yes, it's sentimental and ridiculous and uncool, but so what? Let yourself get crazy happy just because you have another shot at another day, another chance to jump around with the "leaping greenly spirits of trees" under a "blue true dream of sky."

In Blackwater Woods

Look, the trees
are turning
their own bodies
into pillars

of light,
are giving off the rich
fragrance of cinnamon
and fulfillment,

the long tapers
of cattails
are bursting and floating away over
the blue shoulders

of the ponds,
and every pond,
no matter what its
name is, is

nameless now.
Every year

everything
I have ever learned

in my lifetime
leads back to this: the fires
and the black river of loss
whose other side

is salvation,
whose meaning
none of us will ever know.
To live in this world

you must be able
to do three things:
to love what is mortal;
to hold it

against your bones knowing
your own life depends on it;
and, when the time comes to let it go,
to let it go.

MARY OLIVER

The Fish

I caught a tremendous fish
and held him beside the boat
half out of water, with my hook
fast in a corner of his mouth.
He didn't fight.
He hadn't fought at all.
He hung a grunting weight,
battered and venerable
and homely. Here and there
his brown skin hung in strips
like ancient wallpaper,
and its pattern of darker brown
was like wallpaper:
shapes like full-blown roses
stained and lost through age.
He was speckled with barnacles,
fine rosettes of lime,
and infested
with tiny white sea-lice,
and underneath two or three
rags of green weed hung down.

While his gills were breathing in
the terrible oxygen
—the frightening gills,
fresh and crisp with blood,
that can cut so badly—
I thought of the coarse white flesh
packed in like feathers,
the big bones and the little bones,
the dramatic reds and blacks
of his shiny entrails,
and the pink swim-bladder
like a big peony.
I looked into his eyes
which were far larger than mine
but shallower, and yellowed,
the irises backed and packed
with tarnished tinfoil
seen through the lenses
of old scratched isinglass.
They shifted a little, but not
to return my stare.
—It was more like the tipping
of an object toward the light.

I admired his sullen face,
the mechanism of his jaw,
and then I saw
that from his lower lip
—if you could call it a lip—
grim, wet, and weaponlike,
hung five old pieces of fish-line,
or four and a wire leader
with the swivel still attached,
with all their five big hooks
grown firmly in his mouth.
A green line, frayed at the end
where he broke it, two heavier lines,
and a fine black thread
still crimped from the strain and snap
when it broke and he got away.
Like medals with their ribbons
frayed and wavering,
a five-haired beard of wisdom
trailing from his aching jaw.
I stared and stared
and victory filled up
the little rented boat,
from the pool of bilge

where oil had spread a rainbow
around the rusted engine
to the bailer rusted orange,
the sun-cracked thwarts,
the oarlocks on their strings,
the gunnels—until everything
was rainbow, rainbow, rainbow!
And I let the fish go.

ELIZABETH BISHOP

Let Evening Come

Let the light of late afternoon
shine through chinks in the barn, moving
up the bales as the sun moves down.

Let the cricket take up chafing
as a woman takes up her needles
and her yarn. Let evening come.

Let dew collect on the hoe abandoned
in long grass. Let the stars appear
and the moon disclose her silver horn.

Let the fox go back to its sandy den.
Let the wind die down. Let the shed
go black inside. Let evening come.

To the bottle in the ditch, to the scoop
in the oats, to air in the lung
let evening come.

Let it come, as it will, and don't
be afraid. God does not leave us
comfortless, so let evening come.

JANE KENYON

Morning

Why do we bother with the rest of the day,
the swale of the afternoon,
the sudden dip into evening,

then night with his notorious perfumes,
his many-pointed stars?

This is the best—
throwing off the light covers,
feet on the cold floor,
and buzzing around the house on espresso—

maybe a splash of water on the face,
a palmful of vitamins—
but mostly buzzing around the house on espresso,

dictionary and atlas open on the rug,
the typewriter waiting for the key of the head,
a cello on the radio,

and, if necessary, the windows—
trees fifty, a hundred years old
out there,
heavy clouds on the way
and the lawn steaming like a horse
in the early morning.

BILLY COLLINS

Musée des Beaux Arts

About suffering they were never wrong,
The Old Masters: how well they understood
Its human position; how it takes place
While someone else is eating or opening a
      window or just walking dully along;
How, when the aged are reverently, passionately
      waiting
For the miraculous birth, there always must be
Children who did not specially want it to
      happen, skating
On a pond at the edge of the wood:
They never forgot
That even the dreadful martyrdom must run its
      course
Anyhow in a corner, some untidy spot
Where the dogs go on with their doggy life and the
      torturer's horse
Scratches its innocent behind on a tree.

In Brueghel's *Icarus*, for instance: how everything
      turns away
Quite leisurely from the disaster; the
      ploughman may
Have heard the splash, the forsaken cry,
But for him it was not an important failure; the
      sun shone
As it had to on the white legs disappearing into
      the green
Water; and the expensive delicate ship that must
      have seen
Something amazing, a boy falling out of the sky,
Had somewhere to get to and sailed calmly on.

W. H. AUDEN

Tiara

Peter died in a paper tiara
cut from a book of princess paper dolls;
he loved royalty, sashes

and jewels. *I don't know,*
he said, when he woke in the hospice,
*I was watching the Bette Davis film
festival*

on Channel 57 and then—
At the wake, the tension broke
when someone guessed

the casket was closed because
he was *in there in a big wig
and heels*, and someone said,

*You know he's always late,
he probably isn't here yet—
he's still fixing his makeup.*

And someone said he asked for it.
Asked for it—
when all he did was go down

into the salt tide
of wanting as much as he wanted,
giving himself over so drunk

or stoned it almost didn't matter who,
though they were beautiful,
stampeding into him in the simple,

ravishing music of their hurry.
I think heaven is perfect stasis
poised over the realms of desire,

where dreaming and waking men lie
on the grass while wet horses
roam among them, huge fragments

of the music we die into
in the body's paradise.
Sometimes we wake not knowing

how we came to lie here,
or who has crowned us with these
temporary,
precious stones. And given

the world's perfectly turned shoulders,
the deep hollows blued by longing,
given the irreplaceable silk

of horses rippling in orchards,
fruit thundering and chiming down,
given the ordinary marvels of form

and gravity, what could he do,
what could any of us ever do
but ask for it?

MARK DOTY

Upon Entering

I shall die in my boots.
Kick open the saloon doors
of heaven or hell,
lasso the darkest *hombre*
and shoot any hat in the house
who doesn't buy me a drink.

KIM KONOPKA

O Taste and See

The world is
not with us enough.
O taste and see

the subway Bible poster said,
meaning The Lord, meaning
if anything all that lives
to the imagination's tongue,

grief, mercy, language,
tangerine, weather, to
breathe them, bite,
savor, chew, swallow, transform

into our flesh our
deaths, crossing the street, plum, quince,
living in the orchard and being

hungry, and plucking
the fruit.

DENISE LEVERTOV

Strawberrying

My hands are murder-red. Many a plump head
drops on the heap in the basket. Or, ripe
to bursting, they might be hearts, matching
the blackbird's wing-fleck. Gripped to a reed
he shrieks his ko-ka-ree in the next field.
He's left his peck in some juicy cheeks, when
at first blush and mostly white, they showed
streaks of sweetness to the marauder.

We're picking near the shore, the morning
sunny, a slight wind moving rough-veined leaves
our hands rumple among. Fingers find by feel
the ready fruit in clusters. Here and there,
their swishy wounds. . . . Flesh was perfect
yesterday. . . . June was for gorging. . . .
sweet hearts young and firm before decay.

"Take only the biggest, and not too ripe,"
a mother calls to her girl and boy, barefoot
in the furrows. "Don't step on any. Don't
change rows. Don't eat too many." Mesmerized

by the largesse, the children squat and pull
and pick handfuls of rich scarlets, half
for the baskets, half for avid mouths.
Soon, whole faces are stained.

A crop this thick begs for plunder. Ripeness
wants to be ravished, as udders of cows when hard,
the blue-veined bags distended, ache to be
              stripped.
Hunkered in mud between the rows, sun burning
the backs of our necks, we grope for, and rip loose
soft nippled heads. If they bleed—too soft—
let them stay. Let them rot in the heat.

When, hidden away in a damp hollow under
              moldy
leaves, I come upon a clump of heart-shapes
once red, now spiderspit-gray, intact but empty,
still attached to their dead stems—
families smothered as at Pompeii—I rise
and stretch. I eat one more big ripe lopped
head. Red-handed, I leave the field.

MAY SWENSON

Honey

Only calmness will reassure
the bees to let you rob their hoard.
Any sweat of fear provokes them.
Approach with confidence, and from
the side, not shading their entrance.
And hush smoke gently from the spout
of the pot of rags, for sparks will
anger them. If you go near bees
every day they will know you.
And never jerk or turn so quick
you excite them. If weeds are trimmed
around the hive they have access
and feel free. When they taste your smoke
they fill themselves with honey and
are laden and lazy as you
lift the lid to let in daylight.

No bee full of sweetness wants to
sting. Resist greed. With the top off
you touch the fat gold frames, each cell
a hex perfect as a snowflake,
a sealed relic of sun and time
and roots of many acres fixed
in crystal-tight arrays, in rows
and lattices of sweeter latin
from scattered prose of meadow, woods.

ROBERT MORGAN

Teste Moanial

Actually: it's the balls I look for, always.
Men in the street, offices, cars, restaurants,
it's the nuts I imagine—
firm, soft, in hairy sacks
the way they are
down there rigged between the thighs,
the funny way they are.
One in front, a little in front of the other
slightly higher. The way they slip
between your fingers, the way they
slip around in their soft sack.
The way they swing when he walks,
hang down when he bends
over. You see them sometimes bright pink
out of a pair of shorts
when he sits wide and unaware—
the hair sparse and wiry
like that on a poland china pig.

You can see the skin right through—
speckled, with wrinkles like a prune,
but loose, slipping over those kernels
rocking the smooth, small huevos,
so delicate, the cock becomes a diversion,
a masthead overlarge, its flag distracting
from beautiful pebbles beneath.

ANNE MCNAUGHTON

Throw Yourself Like Seed

Shake off this sadness, and recover your spirit;
sluggish you will never see the wheel of fate
that brushes your heel as it turns going by,
the man who wants to live is the man in whom
   life is abundant.

Now you are only giving food to that final pain
which is slowly winding you in the nets of death,
but to live is to work, and the only thing which
   lasts
is the work; start then, turn to the work.

Throw yourself like seed as you walk, and into
   your own field,
don't turn your face for that would be to turn it
   to death,
and do not let the past weigh down your motion.

Leave what's alive in the furrow, what's dead in
    yourself,
for life does not move in the same way as a
    group of clouds;
from your work you will be able one day to
    gather yourself.

MIGUEL DE UNAMUNO

Picnic, Lightning

"My very photogenic mother died in a freak
accident (picnic, lightning) when I was three."
Lolita

It is possible to be struck by a meteor
or a single-engine plane
while reading in a chair at home.
Safes drop from rooftops
and flatten the odd pedestrian
mostly within the panels of the comics,
but still, we know it is possible,
as well as the flash of summer lightning,
the thermos toppling over,
spilling out on the grass.

And we know the message
can be delivered from within.
The heart, no valentine,
decides to quit after lunch,
the power shut off like a switch,
or a tiny dark ship is unmoored
into the flow of the body's rivers,
the brain a monastery,
defenseless on the shore.

This is what I think about
when I shovel compost
into a wheelbarrow,
and when I fill the long flower boxes,
then press into rows
the limp roots of red impatiens—
the instant hand of Death
always ready to burst forth
from the sleeve of his voluminous cloak.

Then the soil is full of marvels,
bits of leaf like flakes off a fresco,
red-brown pine needles, a beetle quick
to burrow back under the loam.

Then the wheelbarrow is a wilder blue,
the clouds a brighter white,

and all I hear is the rasp of the steel edge
against a round stone,
the small plants singing
with lifted faces, and the click
of the sundial
as one hour sweeps into the next.

BILLY COLLINS

Mowing

There was never a sound beside the wood but
      one,
And that was my long scythe whispering to the
      ground.
What was it it whispered? I knew not well myself;
Perhaps it was something about the heat of the
      sun,
Something, perhaps, about the lack of sound—
And that was why it whispered and did not speak.
It was no dream of the gift of idle hours,
Or easy gold at the hand of fey or elf:
Anything more than the truth would have
      seemed too weak
To the earnest love that laid the swale in rows,
Not without feeble-pointed spikes of flowers
(Pale orchises), and scared a bright green snake.
The fact is the sweetest dream that labor knows.
My long scythe whispered and left the hay to
      make.

ROBERT FROST

i thank You God for
most this amazing

i thank You God for most this amazing
day: for the leaping greenly spirits of trees
and a blue true dream of sky; and for everything
which is natural which is infinite which is yes

(i who have died am alive again today,
and this is the sun's birthday; this is the birth
day of life and of love and wings: and of the gay
great happening illimitably earth)

how should tasting touching hearing seeing
breathing any—lifted from the no
of all nothing—human merely being
doubt unimaginable You?

(now the ears of my ears awake and
now the eyes of my eyes are opened)

E. E. CUMMINGS

Afterword

Here you are—you've been to hell and back. You're ready to throw yourself again into this all-too-imperfect world, take pleasure in small everyday delights. Still, don't be surprised if, on a perfect spring day, sipping a perfect cup of coffee, you find yourself scanning the obituaries to see if by any chance he might be dead by now. For a few minutes you might feel the old Rage return; you wish he *would* die just so you would never have to think of him again. You want to wipe him off the earth and out of your head.

If it comes to that, then pick up this book again. Go back and find a poem that matches this feeling, and experience once again that arrow slicing through his shit-filled heart, or that fishhook stuck in your own eye. Studies of recovery from heartbreak suggest that you *will* feel five different emotions on any given day, but as time passes, the "blue true dream of sky" will remain steady, and you will indeed find yourself moving on.

Still, just because you're moving on doesn't mean you're completely cured of heartbreak. Much as we'd like for there to be one surefire route toward getting over it, we're not sure one exists. Our stages of breakup progress aren't intended to be linear milestones ("Oh good, I'm in Real Hope now, so I can kiss Rage good-bye!")—if you're like most of us, you'll find yourself winding in and out of stages. These stages fit *our* experiences (i.e., rage before sadness), but not everyone will feel things in the same order. Some people won't even feel all the stages. We have a friend who seems to go from breakup to Real Hope to Moving On, without any heartache in between. She wanted us to call this book *Hey, Buck Up!* or *Just Get Over It Already!* Another friend has days where she moves from Rage to Sadness to Resolve and back to Rage, all within the space of an hour, and then moves happily through the rest of the day.

It's an imperfect process, getting over loss. If

there's one theme running throughout the poems in each section, it's that the world itself is imperfect and impermanent and flawed. The sky won't stay blue and true, it will inevitably darken. And with every joyous picnic comes the possibility of lightning. Larkin, Olds, and McNaughton invite us to laugh at our own inescapable imperfections; Frost, Yevtushenko, and Glück insist that we understand—happiness cannot exist without pain. And Collins tells us our hearts are not valentines, they're just hearts. They can quit anytime. If you expect "perfect" love you will always be disappointed. Oliver advises instead that we love what is *mortal*, not what is perfect, because only on the other side of the "black river of loss," will we find salvation.

Frankly, we find that a little hard to take. How on earth are we supposed to make our way across that black river of loss? What do we do with our mortal desire for permanent, perfect love—just accept we can't have it? This is where we say turn to poetry. Use it as a bridge to salvation. It's concrete, lasting, and beautiful. It's about as close as we can get to perfection in this world.

Emily Dickinson said, "If I feel physically as if the top of my head were taken off, I know *that* is poetry." Find the poets that blow the top of your head off and read more of their work. We find Collins very accessible, as are Larkin, Bogan, Oliver, Brooks, and Atwood. Glück and Bishop are difficult, but worth the effort. Try tackling Donne and Shakespeare. Don't be intimidated— if you aren't sure what a poem is saying, try to put each line into your own words until you find a meaning that makes sense to you. And share these poems with friends. Try forming a poetry group around this book. Let others help you find meanings you didn't see before.

Remember, we're not promising a miracle cure for heartbreak. But we do believe that poetry provides the comfort of knowing that you're not alone. It shapes your pain and grief into something beautiful and funny and profound. It gives order to the chaos of your feelings and restores your soul— the very same thing that love can do for you.

The only difference is that poetry lasts.

Biographies
of Contributors

YEHUDA AMICHAI (1924–2000): The most translated Hebrew poet in the world. His collections in English include *Open Closed Open* (2000) and *Selected Poetry* (1996).

JOHN ASH (1948–): British poet who moved to New York in 1985 and then to Istanbul in 1996. His most recent books include *Selected Poems* (1996) and *A Byzantine Journey* (1995).

MARGARET ATWOOD (1939–): Canadian novelist and poet. Her second book of poetry, *The Circle Game*, won the Governor General's Award in 1966. She lives in Toronto with her husband and two cats.

W. H. AUDEN (1907–73): One of the most influential poets of the twentieth century, he was born in England but became an American citizen in 1946.

He briefly married a young German woman in order to help her leave Nazi Germany. But after he met Chester Kallman in the United States, the two became lifelong companions.

GWENDOLYN BENNETT (1902–81): Poet, artist, teacher, and journalist, Bennett was an important figure in the Harlem Renaissance, although she never published a collection of poetry. In 1928, she married, moved to Florida, and stopped writing. When her husband died in 1936, she retreated from public life and married a second time.

KATE BINGHAM: Her first novel, *Mummy's Legs*, received an Eric Gregory Award from the Society of Authors. She lives in London.

ELIZABETH BISHOP (1911–79): Highly regarded American poet who won every major poetry award in the United States including the Pulitzer Prize and the National Book Award. She served as Chancellor of the Academy of American Poets from 1966 until 1979. Bishop traveled extensively and spent the last sixteen years of her life in Brazil with her friend and companion, Lota Costellat de Macedo Soares.

LOUISE BOGAN (1897–1970): Influential American poet who won the Bollingen Prize in 1955; she was a poetry critic for *The New Yorker* for thirty-eight years. She was married twice, divorced twice.

WILLIAM EDGAR BOWERS (1924–2000): Bowers was born in Rome, Georgia, and taught at the University of California at Santa Barbara for thirty years. In 1989, he won the Bollingen Prize for poetry. After his mother's death, he moved to San Francisco, where he lived alone.

GWENDOLYN BROOKS (1917–2000): She published her first poems at the age of eleven, was supported, encouraged, and mentored by Langston Hughes, and became the first African-American poet to win the Pulitzer Prize in 1949 for her book *Annie Allen*. She married fellow poet Henry Lowington Blakely in 1939.

MATURI ERUTTALAN CENTAMPUTAN (3rd century A.D.): Indian poet and royal scribe of the Tamilese court. No records exist of his personal life.

SANDRA CISNEROS (1954–): Her work includes four volumes of poetry and the prizewinning *The House On Mango Street*. She lives alone in San Antonio, Texas. She says that men fail to understand that "my center is my writing."

LUCILLE CLIFTON (1936–): Mentored by Sterling Brown at Howard University, she worked as an actor while writing poetry. She was nominated for a Pulitzer Prize in 1980. She won the National Book Award for Poetry in 2001 for *Blessing the Boats: New and Selected Poems, 1988–2000*. She married writer and artist Fred James Clifton in 1958. The couple had six children and remained together until 1984, when Fred Clifton died.

BILLY COLLINS (1941–): According to the *New York Times*, Collins is currently "the most popular poet in America." His four books of poetry have sold more than 50,000 copies. A professor of English at Lehman College, he lives in Westchester County with his wife, Diane.

CAROLYN CREEDON (1969–): Creedon's poem "litany" was included in *The Best American Poetry of 1993*. Creedon works as a waitress in San

Francisco. She quotes Tallulah Bankhead: "I've had a man, and I've had a woman, and there's got to be something better." She recently broke up with her boyfriend.

JUANA INÉS DE LA CRUZ (1651–95): Great poet of Spain's Golden Age and the first person in the Americas to advocate equal rights for women. She was often hired to write love poems by the aristocracy in Mexico. In her thirties, she began a love affair with the wife of the royal governor of Mexico, to whom she wrote extremely erotic love poems. When this relationship ended, she joined a convent, where she died during an outbreak of plague.

E. E. CUMMINGS (1894–1962): Influential American poet known for his experimental, playful style. He was married three times.

EMILY DICKINSON (1830–86): One of the nineteenth century's greatest poets, Dickinson lived quietly at home in Amherst, Massachusetts, with her lawyer father. Although she cultivated intellectual friendships with several men, she never married, and withdrew from social life at twenty-three. Only seven of her approximately one thousand poems were published during her lifetime.

JOHN DONNE (1572–1631): British author of religious poems and essays as well as some astonishingly erotic love poetry, Donne secretly married "above" himself in 1601. This marriage, considered a criminal act in class-conscious England (Donne was briefly imprisoned), lasted for fifteen years until his wife died giving birth to their twelfth child. After her death, Donne took orders in the church of England and devoted himself to writing holy sonnets.

MARK DOTY (1953–): Contemporary American poet who has won the National Book Critics Circle Award and the T. S. Eliot Prize. His most recent work is *Murano: Poem*. Doty has written extensively about the death of his lover from AIDS.

MICHAEL DRAYTON (1563–1631): British poet who wrote satires, odes, and sonnets. Little information is available about his personal life, but we do know that he wrote a famous series of love poems based on historical figures in England.

MICHAEL FRIED (1939–): A poet and art critic who teaches in the Humanities Center at Johns Hopkins University. He lives in Baltimore.

ROBERT FROST (1874–1963): Considered one of America's greatest poets, he won the Pulitzer Prize four times and read a poem at the inauguration of President John F. Kennedy. As a twenty-year-old, he wandered the Great Dismal Swamp in Virginia to recover from a broken heart. He was married to Elinor White, with whom he had six children.

LOUISE GLÜCK (1943–): American poet whose collections have won both the Pulitzer Prize (1992) and the National Book Critics Circle Award (1985). She lives in Cambridge, Massachusetts, and teaches at Williams College. Glück is divorced.

MARILYN HACKER (1942–): Author of seven books of poetry, she received the National Book Award for *Presentation Piece* in 1975 and the Lambda Award for two other collections. Briefly married, she currently lives with longtime companion Karyn London in New York City and Paris.

JANE HIRSHFIELD (1953–): American poet who studied at the San Francisco Zen Center for eight years. She has translated several collections of Japanese poetry. Her latest works include *The October Palace* and *The Lives of the Heart*.

A. E. HOUSMAN (1859–1936): Educated at Oxford, the brilliant scholar failed his exams there and worked for ten years as a Patent Office Clerk in London. He spent most of his life in love with fellow Oxford student Moses Jackson, but when Jackson married in 1897, Housman was inspired to write poetry. His love for Jackson was the inspiration for many of his poems. His collection of poems *A Shropshire Lad* is his most well-known work.

GEORGIA DOUGLAS JOHNSON (1880–1966): The most famous woman poet of the Harlem Renaissance literary movement, she didn't publish her first poem until she was thirty-six. She married lawyer Henry Lincoln Johnson in 1903—he expected her to be a full-time mother and housekeeper. He died in 1924, and she did not remarry.

JANE KENYON (1947–95): She published four volumes of poetry, including *Constance* (1993). She married fellow poet Donald Hall in 1972. The two lived at Eagle Pond Farm in New Hampshire until her death from leukemia in 1995.

GALWAY KINNELL (1927–): Kinnell has won both the National Book Award and the Pulitzer Prize for Poetry. He is divorced and currently teaches at New York University.

KIM KONOPKA: Her poems have won several awards and have been extensively anthologized. She writes and teaches in Santa Fe, New Mexico. She is currently single, but madly in love with the handsome poet who whispered to her, "Never fall in love with a poet." (And not even the handsome poet knows her date of birth.)

STEVE KOWIT (1938–): Translator of Pablo Neruda's political poetry, Kowit has written two collections of love poems and has taught poetry workshops for over twenty years. He is the author of *In The Palm of Your Hand: The Poet's Portable Workshop*. He currently teaches at Southwestern College and lives in the California backcountry.

PHILLIP LARKIN (1922–85): British novelist and poet who said about himself: "One of those old-type natural fouled-up guys." He never married.

DENISE LEVERTOV (1923–97): British-born American poet, editor, and political activist, Levertov wrote thirty books of poetry, many with political and antiwar themes. She married Mitchell Goodman, an American writer, in 1948.

ANNE MCNAUGHTON (1945–): McNaughton lives in Taos, New Mexico, where she and her husband, Peter Rabbit, conduct the annual Taos Poetry Circus. The two have been married, divorced, and remarried.

ALICE MEYNELL (1847–1922): British poet and essayist. She married author and editor Wilfred Meynell in 1877; he was attracted first to her poetry and then to her.

EDWIN MORGAN (1920–): Born in Edinburgh, Morgan has lived and taught in Glasgow most of his life. Considered one of Scotland's greatest poets (and an accomplished linguist), he has won the Royal Bank of Scotland Book of the Year

Award, the Soros Translation Award, and the Stakis Prize for Scottish Writer of the Year (1998).

ROBERT MORGAN (1944–): Novelist and poet, he has received four NEA fellowships and the North Carolina Award for Literature. Since 1992, he has been the Kappa Alpha professor of English at Cornell University.

HOWARD MOSS (1922–87): American poet, playwright, and poetry editor of *The New Yorker* magazine for nearly forty years.

PABLO NERUDA (1904–73): Nobel Prize–winning Chilean poet. He received the Lenin Peace Prize in 1953. He was married three times—the last (and most successful) marriage was to Chilean singer Matilda Urrutea.

SHARON OLDS (1942–): Often described as a confessional poet, Olds won the National Book Critics' Circle Award for *The Dead and the Living* in 1983. She teaches poetry workshops at New York University and Goldwater Hospital. She lives in New York City and is fiercely protective of her private life.

MARY OLIVER (1935–): Oliver has won both the Pulitzer Prize (1984) for *American Primitive* and the National Book Award (1992) for *New and Selected Poems*. She lives in Provincetown, Massachusetts.

DOROTHY PARKER (1893–1967): Journalist and humorist, and a founding member of the famous Algonquin Round Table. After divorcing her first husband, Edwin Parker, she married fellow writer Alan Campbell, with whom she worked as a screenwriter. During the 1920s, she fought with her husband, drank heavily, and attempted suicide several times. She wrote her own epitaph: "Pardon my dust," and left her entire estate to Martin Luther King, Jr.

COVENTRY PATMORE (1823–96): Popular Victorian poet who wrote "The Angel in the House," an homage to married life and his wife, Emily. Unfortunately, after six children and fifteen years, the "ideal" wife died. Two years later, Patmore married his second wife, and when she died in 1880, he quickly married his children's governess.

MARGE PIERCY (1936–): Novelist and poet, Piercy was active in antiwar politics and the women's liberation movement during the 1960s. She presently lives in Cape Cod with her third husband.

MARIE PONSOT (1921–): Author of several collections of poetry, she married painter Claude Ponsot in Paris. After he left her, she spent the next twenty-five years raising their seven children. She currently teaches at Columbia, and her most recent collection of poetry is *The Bird Catcher*.

WILLIAM SHAKESPEARE (1564–1616): Still believed by many to be the greatest writer in the English language, Shakespeare married Anne Hathaway (who was eight years older than he) in November of 1582. Their first child arrived just seven months later. Even though he stayed married to Hathaway for the rest of his life and maintained a home for his family in Stratford, Shakespeare acted, lived, and wrote in London. Unfortunately, little is known about his personal life there.

TOM SIMON (1951–): Editor of *Poetry Under Oath*, Simon is a book-selling executive who says he "knows a good laugh when he sees one." He lives in Brooklyn with his wife and three children.

JOSEPH STROUD (1943–): Has published three volumes of poetry; his latest work is *Below Cold Mountain*. He lives in a cabin in the Sierra Nevada and in Santa Cruz, California.

MAY SWENSON (1919–89): American poet and editor, she was a Chancellor of the Academy of American Poets from 1980 to 1989. Her works include *To Mix With Time* and *May Out West*. She never married.

WISLAWA SZYMBORSKA (1923–): Polish poet who won the Nobel Prize in 1996. She was married twice and is now a widow living in Krakow.

NORMA TILDEN (1943–): Teaches at Georgetown University, has published in *The Lyric* and *Thought and Action*. When she was three, a boy cousin informed her that all dogs were male. She has sometimes lived without a man, but never without a dog.

MIGUEL DE UNAMUNO (1864–1936): Spanish writer, philosopher, and political activist. He married Concepcion Lizarraga Ecennaro in 1891—they had ten children.

ELIZABETH ASH VÉLEZ (1945–): Journalist and writer, Vélez teaches at Georgetown University. She has two sons and has been married for thirty-two years.

LARRY VÉLEZ (1945–): Journalist and writer. He currently writes speeches in Washington, D.C., where he lives with his wife of thirty-two years.

DEREK WALCOTT (1930–): Saint Lucian poet and playwright who won the Nobel Prize for Literature in 1992. So far, he has been married three times.

WILLIAM CARLOS WILLIAMS (1883–1963): Winner of both the National Book Award and the Pulitzer Prize, Williams lived with his wife in Rutherford, New Jersey, where he practiced pediatric medicine. (Among his young patients was poet Allen Ginsberg.)

JAMES WRIGHT (1927–80): Highly regarded American poet who won the Pulitzer Prize in 1966. He was married twice.

WILLIAM BUTLER YEATS (1865–1939): Considered the greatest of Irish poets, he received the Nobel Prize for Literature in 1923. Although he was married in 1917, Maude Gonne, the beautiful Irish revolutionary, inspired many of his love poems. (It was unrequited love for Yeats, apparently.)

YEVGENY YEVTUSHENKO (1933–): Well-known Russian poet of the post-Stalin generation. A vocal critic of communism, he has been married four times.

Acknowledgments

Special thanks to Andrew Carroll of the American Poetry and Literacy Project, Georgetown University, Lisa Mezzetti, and our friends at the Plaza Hotel in Las Vegas, NM. We would also like to thank our editors, Molly Chehak and Caryn Karmatz Rudy, and our agent, Miriam Altshuler.

Elizabeth gratefully acknowledges the love and support of husband Larry and sons Stephen and Nicholas. And Mary thanks Greg for bringing a new kind of poetry to her life.

About the Editors

MARY D. ESSELMAN is a teacher and freelance writer currently working in public television. She is a former *People* magazine correspondent and Georgetown University instructor of English and women's studies. During the course of writing this book, she met—and married—her husband.

ELIZABETH ASH VÉLEZ is academic coordinator of the Community Scholars Program at Georgetown University, where she also teaches women's studies and nonfiction writing. She is a published poet and a regular *People* magazine correspondent. Vélez just celebrated her thirty-second wedding anniversary.

A Book of
PRAYERS
for Young
Women

STORMIE OMARTIAN
PAIGE OMARTIAN

HARVEST HOUSE PUBLISHERS
EUGENE, OREGON

Cover by Koechel Peterson & Associates, Inc., Minneapolis, Minnesota

Cover illustrations © Thinkstock

A BOOK OF PRAYERS FOR YOUNG WOMEN

Copyright © 2013 by Stormie Omartian and Paige Omartian
Published by Harvest House Publishers
Eugene, Oregon 97402
www.harvesthousepublishers.com
ISBN 978-0-7369-5360-3
ISBN 978-0-7369-5361-0 (eBook)

Printed in China

14 15 16 17 18 19 20 21 / RDS-JH / 10 9 8 7 6 5 4 3 2

Contents

Why We Wrote This Book Together

1. Lord, Help Me Seek You
2. Rejecting the Fear of Rejection
3. I Want to Be Beautiful
4. Trusting God in Times of Loss
5. Feeling Obsessed with Planning
6. Seeing Things from God's Perspective
7. I Don't Feel Good Enough
8. Surrendering My Life to the Lord
9. I Am Your Servant
10. When I Need to Forgive
11. I Just Want Love
12. Help Me Separate Myself from Sin
13. I Need Godly Friends
14. Finding My Identity in the Lord
15. I Feel Like a Failure
16. Showing Love to Others
17. Purpose in My Imperfections
18. When I Feel Anxious
19. Lord, Use Me to Change the World
20. Getting Close to God
21. Help Me Not to Compromise

22. Sometimes It's Hard for Me to Pray
23. I Escape to You
24. When I Am Discouraged
25. Reclaim What I've Lost
26. I Am Created for Good Things
27. Lord, Guide My Choices
28. Speaking Words That Please God
29. Being a Woman of Integrity
30. Refusing Negative Thoughts About Myself
31. I Need a Reality Check
32. When Life Seems Overwhelming
33. You Are My Father
34. When My Heart Is Distressed
35. Storing My Treasures in Heaven
36. Taking Control of My Thoughts
37. I Feel Hopeless
38. Praising God No Matter What Happens
39. Waiting for My Husband
40. Moving into the Future God Has for Me
41. Lord, Give Me Wisdom
42. How Do I See Answers to My Prayers?
43. Forgiving Myself
44. Establishing Right Priorities
45. Lord, Reveal My Pride
46. When I Don't Feel Good About Myself

47. Give Me Discernment

48. Living with a Grateful Heart

49. Lord, Show Me My Spiritual Gifts

50. Choosing to Walk in the Spirit

51. Respecting Myself

52. Praying for Difficult People

53. Give Me True Faith

54. Not Letting Emotions Rule My Day

55. Lord, Give Me Confidence

56. Rising Above Peer Pressure

57. Seeing Myself Through God's Eyes

58. When My Prayers Have Not Been Answered

59. Ignite My Passion

60. Mending a Broken Heart

61. Lord, Help Me Be Pure

62. Staying Free of Envy

63. Lord, I Need Healing

64. I Don't Want to Live in Fear

65. What Is True Love?

66. Understanding My Purpose

67. Teach Me to Make Disciples

68. Bearing Good Fruit

69. Promises in My Pain

70. Resisting Temptation

71. I Am Your Ambassador

72. Refusing to Be Desperate
73. Lord, Guard My Heart
74. Making Wise Decisions
75. Take Away My Anger
76. Staying Strong in Difficult Times
77. Keep My Eyes on You
78. I'm Concerned About My Safety
79. Help Me to Be a Listener
80. Purify My Thoughts
81. I Don't Feel Adequate to Your Call
82. Faith to Believe for the Impossible
83. Show Me How to Use My Life
84. The Hardest Thing About Prayer
85. Purify My Mind, Mouth, and Heart
86. Refusing to Feel Worthless
87. Help Me Not to Judge Others
88. Finding God's Will for My Life
89. I'm Here for a Reason
90. Seeing My Body as Precious
91. Lord, You Are Unchanging
92. Guide Me in the Right Direction
93. Strengthen My Heart Against Temptation
94. Choosing a New Beginning
95. Show Me My Purpose
96. Finding Freedom in the Lord

97.	I Feel Alone
98.	Living a Holy Life
99.	Facing Troubles and Hard Times
100.	Seeking True Success
101.	Lord, I Long to Be Close to You
102.	When I Feel Powerless
103.	Save Me from My Pity Parties
104.	How Can I Make a Difference?
105.	Feeling Out of Place
106.	When I Want to Give Up
107.	Waiting on My Future
108.	I Have Unfulfilled Dreams
109.	Finding Your Strength in My Weakness
110.	Seeing God's Light in Dark Times
111.	When I Feel Shame
112.	I Want to Be a Whole Person
113.	I Am Cherished
114.	How Do I Honor My Parents?
115.	I Feel So Restless
116.	Will God Provide for Me?
117.	Lord, Test My Heart
118.	Finding Favor with God and Others
119.	Preserve My Reputation
120.	Welcoming God's Presence
121.	Consume Me with Your Fire

122. Saving Good Relationships
123. Starving for Redemption
124. When Everything Is Going Right
125. Lord, Help Me Be Real
126. Give Me a Right Heart
127. Lord, Don't Let Me Be Lukewarm
128. Making Hope a Habit
129. God, You Really Want to Use *Me*?
130. Prayer That Makes a Difference
131. Teach Me to Be Gracious
132. Staying Free of Destructive Relationships
133. I Return to You
134. Identifying My Enemy
135. On the Edge of Rebellion
136. Learning to Pray First
137. I'd Rather Be with You Than Anywhere
138. Not Letting Others Define Who I Am
139. I Feel So Insecure
140. Praying with Other People
141. Lord, I'm Afraid
142. You're All That I Need
143. Lord, Save My Loved One
144. Embracing the Moment
145. Drama with Friends
146. Praying for My Country

147.   Lord, Send Me a Mentor

148.   Getting Free of Addictions

149.   Prayer for a Suicidal Friend

150.   Help Me Understand the Bible

151.   Restoration with Parents

152.   Worshipping God *His* Way

153.   I Want to Be a Light

154.   Transforming My Life

Why We Wrote
This Book Together

STORMIE

My teens and twenties were the most difficult years of my life. And they didn't have to be. But I didn't know that then. I made a lot of wrong choices and paid a heavy price for them because I didn't know how to navigate my circumstances. I thought things just happened to me and I had no control over them. But nothing could be further from the truth.

I lived with depression, anxiety, fear, hopelessness, and constant problems that I struggled to overcome or tried to hide. I now know that those early years can be inspiring, fun, and productive, and become the foundation for a life of purpose and success. That foundation is laid in a relationship with God through Jesus, His Son, and in communication with Him through prayer. I didn't discover all that until I was 28 years old and wanted to end my life because I couldn't live with the pain I felt any longer. But a friend took me to meet her pastor and he led me to the Lord.

Since that time I have come to understand who

God is and what He wants to do in our lives. And He wants to do far more than we think. Now I want everyone to know God. I want to help people walk closely with Him by learning to pray. I want as many people as possible to understand how the amazing power of prayer affects not only their own lives, but also the lives of other people and situations.

I have written over fifty books on prayer but I have not written a prayer book specifically for young women until now. And it has long been on my heart to do so. But now I have the perfect writing partner for this book. When I first met Paige, it was before I even dreamed she would become my daughter-in-law. I was immediately impressed by how she, at such a young age, was wise beyond her years. She was nineteen at the time and had survived a traumatic near-death experience at eleven years old. In that experience God gave her a new perspective on life and the desire to help others in her generation gain that same perspective without having to go through a traumatic experience themselves. She is a great example of how God uses the difficult things in our lives for good.

Paige had recorded an album that my son, Christopher, produced. That is how he met her. She was also working on a television show for young people and through that I saw that she is an excellent communicator—very natural, passionate, and heartfelt. When

I told her she should write a book about her amazing life experience she said she had already started writing it. She let me read what she had written, and I thought it was excellent and needed to be published. I recommended her to my publisher, Harvest House Publishers, and they agreed that she was writing something that must be read by young people everywhere. The result is her book *Wake Up, Generation*. If you have not read it, I highly recommend that you do for I know it will inspire you to great things in your life. It did that for me.

After that book came out, Harvest House Publishers asked Paige and me to cowrite this book of prayers for young women because we each have a specific perspective that we bring to it. We each have written seventy-two prayers. I have written mine from the standpoint of a mentor to you. These are prayers I wish I had known to pray when I was your age because I could have spared myself so much grief. But I can now give them to you so you will have the benefit of that knowledge and experience without having to pay the price I did for not knowing. Paige knows what the specific needs of your generation are and the situations and challenges that you uniquely and commonly face today. She applies that knowledge to her prayers along with a passionate concern for the men and women of her generation. Paige has a tremendous heart for the Lord because she has faced the enemy of death and by the power of God has won. She can help you face the challenges of *your* life and win too. As you read on, I know you will love and appreciate her as I do.

PAIGE

The first time I met Stormie was when she came to dinner with her son, Chris, and me at our favorite Japanese restaurant. I had heard many great things about her, but had no idea how great until I met her. Stormie's presence and spirit instantly made me feel loved, safe, and like I had known her for years. There was hardly a pause in our conversation the whole night, except when we absolutely had to chew. One of the things that struck me that night was the way that she would humorously make light of herself, revealing a captivating humility that I adored. I couldn't believe the way my heart felt at home.

Chris and I married on November 11, 2011, and it was truly the most profound and incredible day of my life. Not only did the Lord so graciously give me the man of my dreams whom I've prayed for my whole life…but He gave me an amazing family along with him! I cannot believe God's goodness to me. Now that Stormie is my second mom, I've had the privilege of witnessing what a woman of God she is daily. Even when she's finishing her latest book, preparing for a speaking event, and keeping her own household running, she still remembers an item I once mentioned I needed and calls to let me know she's found it and it's being delivered. There are not many people who care about others the way she does. I believe this is a huge reason why her books have been so successful and powerful. She truly cares about you.

When Stormie called me a few months ago to let me know that Harvest House Publishers would like us to write this book together, my end of the phone line went silent. To say that I was intimidated to write this book with her is an understatement. Stormie has written more books than I can count and is known for the beautiful and life-changing way that she leads people to deepen their walk with the Lord in prayer. While God has done miraculous things in my life and allowed me to have my first book published, there's no need to explain the difference between our experience and positions. Though I had no idea what I had to offer, I felt like God was calling me to accept and journey with her in the writing of this book. I trusted that God knew my inadequacies far better than I did and would provide!

Unexpectedly, my own prayer life was attacked as I began writing. I began to question whether my prayers were truly powerful, and wondered who I was to be writing prayers that others would then pray themselves. As my husband, family, and friends prayed over me, I began to see the attack for what it was… the enemy trying to stop me. My prayers aren't powerful because I have some special wording. They are powerful because I have faith and the Holy Spirit is in me, leading me to speak to the Father about the real things I'm facing. If Christ is in you, you have that power too.

In this book you'll find insight from two similar but very different perspectives. Stormie understands where you are. Her story is unbelievable and she knows the battles you face in the most extreme way. She is able to zoom out with the wisdom her years have brought to not only understand the negative effects these circumstances have had on her life, but also how we each can pray in order to avoid those consequences in our lives.

I am in the midst of this "young woman-ness" with you. I know what I face and what my friends face. Before I wrote each prayer, I prayed for you first, asking that the Lord would show me the words He longs to hear from His daughters. My heart and intent with each prayer is for you to know how real you can be with God. I've been beautifully surprised and comforted to learn that the Lord desires a messy love relationship with us. This means that He doesn't want your polished words—He wants the raw and real you. He desires to be closer to you than anyone else in your life. When we begin to open our hearts and be vulnerable with God, we receive more from Him than we could ever hope for, expect, or imagine. Your prayers are powerful. Believe, watch, and be amazed.

STORMIE AND PAIGE

With all that being said, we hope you will find this book a great help to you. You can start at the beginning and read it straight through—one or more prayers every day—or you can skip around to whatever prayer topics seem most important to you at the time. Whichever way you approach it, it is important to eventually read every prayer, because together they will cover your life in the way it needs to be covered—with no important aspects left out. There is no right or wrong way to do it; there is only your way as the Holy Spirit leads you. We pray that each prayer in this book will be a starting point from which you will share your own specific needs at that moment with the Lord.

One last thing we want you to know is that we love you, our dear reader and sister in the Lord, and we pray you will be greatly touched by God's life-changing power in response to your prayers and that you will establish a strong and life-changing walk with God.

1

Lord, Help Me Seek You

*You will seek me and find me when you
seek me with all your heart.*

JEREMIAH 29:13

Heavenly Father, earnestly I seek You. I put aside everything and count You as more valuable, more precious to me than anything in all creation. Lord, You are here with me always, yet You promise that as I draw near to You, You will draw nearer to me (James 4:8). Your presence is worth giving up all else. Don't let me start my days without seeking You and submitting myself to the guidance of Your Holy Spirit.

Forgive me for all the times I haven't sought You because somehow I thought I was better off on my own. What a tragedy not to seek You and to leave the treasures of Your goodness untouched as though they were not worth finding. If I had only understood my own condition, I would have been on my face before You constantly. Give me a heart that longs to know You and love You deeply. I need You more than the air I breathe—for You are life itself.

In Jesus' name I pray.

—*Paige*

2

Rejecting the Fear of Rejection

The LORD will not reject his people.

PSALM 94:14

Dear Lord, help me to not be influenced by fear that I will be rejected. I don't want that feeling to blind me to the actual truth of my situation. I know that probably everyone is rejected by someone at one time or another. But I don't want the fear of that to control my life. When I am rejected—or *feel* rejected—make me strong in my mind and heart so I will not be brought down by it. Help me to remember that I am always accepted in Your eyes. Thank You, Lord, that You have *chosen* me to be Your child and You will never reject me.

Where I have deep hurts because of rejection in the past, I pray You would heal those wounds. Enable me to no longer live in the pain of rejection, for You are *with* me to *help* and *strengthen* me (Isaiah 41:9-10). Thank You that You love me the way I am, yet You help me every day to become more like You. Teach me to accept myself the way You unconditionally accept me.

In Jesus' name I pray.

—*Stormie*

3

I Want to Be Beautiful

Your beauty…should be that of your inner
self, the unfading beauty of a gentle and quiet
spirit, which is of great worth in God's sight.

1 PETER 3:3-4

Jesus, I want to be beautiful. I know this desire is of You because You long to reveal Your beauty through us. I love that You've placed Your gentleness, sensitive Spirit, compassion, and beauty in the heart of women. Who I am is a direct reflection of gorgeous qualities of You. I pray You would reveal Your beauty in me and that for once I would *believe* that it has nothing to do with my outward appearance. I'm so hung up on that, Lord.

You created my eyes not to allure, but to *see* evidence of You in a world in need. My ears were created to *hear* Your voice and the testimonies of Your people. My lips were created to proclaim You—to *speak* words of life and encouragement. My hands were created to *touch* the world and live out the purpose You've given me. My body was created to be the temple of Your Holy Spirit. Lord, You created beauty, so only You define it.

In Jesus' name I pray.

—*Paige*

4

Trusting God in Times of Loss

Blessed are those who mourn, for they will be comforted.

MATTHEW 5:4

Dear Lord Jesus, I thank You that no matter what I have lost in my life—whether it is a person, a relationship, a much-loved pet, finances, a valued object, an opportunity, or an ability to do something—You know the pain I feel because of it. Only by Your Holy Spirit in me—the Comforter whom You sent to uphold us—can I be made to rise above my grief. Because of You I don't have to hurt forever and I can feel complete again.

I pray that the hole I feel in my heart because of a loss I have suffered will be filled with Your love, peace, and joy. I know that You, Lord, are good and if I walk day by day with You, this seemingly unending pain will actually fade away and I will find happiness again. I choose to walk step-by-step with You today, trusting You to help me face any loss I have experienced with renewed hope about the future. Thank You that You fill every empty place in me.

In Jesus' name I pray.

—*Stormie*

5

Feeling Obsessed with Planning

Many are the plans in a person's heart, but it is the LORD's purpose that prevails.

PROVERBS 19:21

Lord, I need to slow down. I've been running ahead making so many plans that my head is spinning. I always think if I can just plan "this" and have control of "that" everything will run much smoother. But I realize why this isn't working…because I've left *You* out. Forgive me for my need to control and teach me how to let You lead. You are God, and I am not. I realize that when I try to take the reins I am basically saying, "I know better than You, God!" I repent of this and declare my trust in Your divine Plan.

Father, I come to You today and scrap my plans. Yes, there are things to do and work to be done, but I lay down my own schedule and agenda. Where are *You* going today, Lord? I want to follow. Who are *You* touching? I want to reach them. What do *You* desire to accomplish by the end of this day? I want to be a part. Lord, I cast aside my plans today because I'd rather follow *Yours*.

In Jesus' name I pray.

—Paige

6

Seeing Things from God's Perspective

Open my eyes that I may see wonderful things in your law.
PSALM 119:18

Dear Lord, help me to always be able to see what is right and good about my life instead of thinking about what is wrong. Sometimes when things don't turn out like I planned, hoped, or prayed they would, I start to have doubts about myself instead of believing that You are doing something good in the situation. I don't want to be worrying about what has happened—or not happened—when actually I should be looking to You and thanking You that You can turn it around for good.

I believe that You are a good God and that You have the best for me. Help me to see Your good in every situation. Your Word says that everyone who takes refuge in You will be blessed (Psalm 34:8). I trust in You and in Your Word and thank You for the blessings You are pouring out on my life. Open my eyes so that I can see things from Your perspective. Help me to see the whole truth of what You are doing in my life.

In Jesus' name I pray.

—*Stormie*

7

I Don't Feel Good Enough

Trust in him at all times…pour out your
hearts to him, for God is our refuge.

PSALM 62:8

Father, today I just want to put a bag over my head and hide. I don't feel pretty, put together, or worth anyone's time. Everywhere I turn I'm plagued by the overwhelming feeling that *I'm not good enough*. It seems I'm either too little or too much…but not enough. Jesus, with a desperate heart I come to You needing Your arms to hold me. I'm struggling with doubt that You even want to hear my prayer, but I cling to Your Word that tells me to trust You and pour out my heart.

In Your name, I stand against the feelings of worthlessness that have stolen Your joy and peace in my life. Lift off the lies that weigh so heavily on me, and replace them with your glorious Truth. Your Word says that I am precious and honored in Your sight…and that *You love me* (Isaiah 43:4). You call me Your chosen one in whom You delight (Isaiah 42:1)! I claim these words knowing they have the power to transform my life.

In Jesus' name I pray.

—Paige

Surrendering My Life to the Lord

Humble yourselves under the mighty hand of God, that He may exalt you in due time, casting all your care upon Him, for He cares for you.

1 PETER 5:6-7 NKJV

Lord, I pray that You will rule over every area of my life. Help me to fully trust You with my whole heart and mind. Teach me to obey You in all things and not try to live life my own way and on my own terms. I surrender my life to You. I give You my work, my relationships, my activities, my interests, and my goals. I put everything in Your hands so it can be used for Your glory.

I don't want to live according to my own desires, but instead I want to do what *You* want. I come humbly before You knowing that as I do You will lift me up. I give my concerns to You and thank You that You care about each one because You care about me. Thank You for Your love and the blessings that You pour out on me every day.

In Jesus' name I pray.

—*Stormie*

9

I Am Your Servant

Then I heard the voice of the Lord saying,
"Whom shall I send? And who will go for
us?" And I said, "Here am I. Send me!"

ISAIAH 6:8

Jesus, I am Your servant. I serve such a Good Master. My soul burns to be used by You as I long to fulfill the purpose You've given me. I cast aside fear and whole-heartedly submit my life and dreams to You, because I know Your plan is best for me. You're the only Master whose slaves become free when they submit to You. I thirst to put a smile on Your face and be a light in this dark world.

My body is a jar of clay, yet You've laid treasures inside of it to show the world that this all-surpassing power is from You and not me (2 Corinthians 4:7). Use me as a vessel to pour out Your love and truth on everyone I encounter. I make myself available to You. You've said that the harvest is plentiful but the workers are few (Luke 10:2). I declare myself a worker for Your Kingdom, a servant to Your throne. May the cry of my heart forever be, *"Here am I. Send me!"*

In Jesus' name I pray.

—*Paige*

10

When I Need to Forgive

*But if you do not forgive others their sins, your
Father will not forgive your sins.*

MATTHEW 6:15

Heavenly Father, help me to forgive others the way
You have commanded me in Your Word. I know that
forgiving someone is a choice I must make and I choose
right now to be a forgiving person. I know I must *decide*
to forgive before I can ever *feel* forgiveness. I confess to
You any unforgiveness I have in me and ask You to set
me free from it.

Show me if there is any lack of forgiveness in me
that I am not seeing. I know that forgiving someone
doesn't make them right, or justify what they have done,
but it frees me from the destruction of bitterness that
not forgiving someone causes. Enable me to forgive
that person whether they apologize or not. Help me to
forgive others so that You will forgive me. I don't want
to limit the good things You want to pour into my life
all because I will not forgive. I never want anything to
come between You and me.

In Jesus' name I pray.

—*Stormie*

11

I Just Want Love

I will betroth you to me forever; I will betroth you in righteousness and justice, in love and compassion.

HOSEA 2:19

Lord, I am feeling heartsick today…heartsick for love. My romantic thoughts have been running away with me, and I just can't stop longing for the right guy's affection and love. I lift my desires up to You because I know You will fulfill them in Your perfect time. *You* are so romantic, Lord. You are the Author of love. When I think of how You laid down Your life for me…there is nothing more You could have done to prove Your extravagant love.

In the book of Hosea, You call a faithful man to marry a prostitute just to exemplify the way that You are a reckless Lover who has been betrayed by us. Could it be that this deep desire for intimacy in my heart can only be filled by You? What lover could compare? Isaiah 54:5 says, "Your Maker is your husband," so Lord, I am betrothed to You. You have loved me with an everlasting love (Jeremiah 31:3) and nothing on earth can measure up. I love You, Jesus. You captivate me. My heart is forever Yours.

In Jesus' name I pray.

—*Paige*

12

Help Me Separate Myself from Sin

No one who lives in him keeps on sinning. No one who continues to sin has either seen him or known him.

1 John 3:6

Dear God, I know that You hate sin (Proverbs 6:16). I hate it too. I hate it enough to completely separate myself from it. I know that any sin in my life grieves Your Holy Spirit and I don't ever want to do that. But I need Your help. So I ask You to give me strong conviction in my soul if ever I am drawn toward any kind of action or thought that goes against Your ways. Your Word says that sin kills, but Your Spirit gives life (Romans 8:2). I choose You and Your ways. I choose life by the power of Your Spirit in me.

Make me aware whenever I am in danger of disobeying Your laws. Only You can enable me to give up all desire for something or someone that goes against Your will for me. Line up the desires of my heart with the desires of Your heart. Help me to separate myself from anything that separates me from You.

In Jesus' name I pray.

—*Stormie*

13

I Need Godly Friends

*One who loves a pure heart and who speaks
with grace will have the king for a friend.*

PROVERBS 22:11

Father, I come before You and ask that You would
bring godly friends into my life. I have seen the influ-
ence that those I spend my time around have on me, and
know that I need to be discerning. You desire for us to
have close fellowship with other believers so I ask for this
in faith, knowing that it's Your will for me to receive this.

I pray that Your Holy Spirit would lead me to the
right people who are also seeking to find godly friend-
ship. You use our relationships to shape, challenge, and
refine us, and I look forward to that growth. Help me,
first of all, to be the kind of friend that I desire to find.
Weed out any bitter roots in me that would repel oth-
ers from trusting me or getting close. Make my words
gracious, my ears eager to listen, my spirit discerning,
and my heart open to love. I wait in earnest expecta-
tion, thanking You in advance for the treasures of godly
friendship that will soon be mine.

In Jesus' name I pray.

—*Paige*

14

Finding My Identity in the Lord

For the pagans run after all these things, and your heavenly Father knows that you need them.

MATTHEW 6:32

Heavenly Father, I thank You that I am Your daughter. Help me to live like the daughter of a King. I don't want to fall into the pride, lure, and lust of the world that steals away the good life You have for me. I want to be full of Your Spirit and not full of myself. Show me how to be Your light in this world without being drawn into what is dark. Thank You that You know my deepest needs.

Enable me to keep my identity in You and who You made me to be. Keep me from giving in to the practices of this culture that are not pleasing to You. Help me to turn away from anything that is polluting my mind and distracting me from all You have for me. I don't want to become accustomed to seeing or doing things that are not right in Your eyes. Thank You for knowing what I need even before *I* do.

In Jesus' name I pray.

—*Stormie*

15

I Feel Like a Failure

Let us throw off everything that hinders and the sin that so easily entangles. And let us run with perseverance the race marked out for us.

HEBREWS 12:1

Heavenly Father, You know how frustrated I am at myself. I feel like a failure. I know my struggles, yet I can't seem to fix them or make them better. Father, You are the Redeemer of all things. Please redeem what I have lost because of my failures. I surrender to You with raised hands, declaring that I am no longer going forward in my own strength. I don't have the power to change on my own so I call upon Your Holy Spirit to transform me.

Your Word says to throw off everything that hinders, so Lord, I cast off all that's been entangling me. Show me what I need to get rid of or stop doing so that I can start doing the things that You've called me to do. In Jesus' name, please help me to overcome (specific area of weakness). Thank You that Your Word says we are more than conquerors through You who love us (Romans 8:37)! Because of You, the victory is already mine.

In Jesus' name I pray.

—*Paige*

16

Showing Love to Others

My command is this: Love each other as I have loved you.

JOHN 15:12

Dear Jesus, help me to love others the way that You do. I know that You love them unconditionally, no matter how they act or what they have done. I find it hard to always do that. You have commanded us to love You and love others, but I find it far easier to love You than I do to love them. Other people fail me and You never do. Other people can be unloving and You never are. That's why I need *Your* love to fill my heart every day.

Thank You that You are the God of love—You don't just *have* love, You *are* love. I pray that Your Spirit of love in me will flow out of me to others like a river. Enable me to show love even to those who are hard to love. Teach me how to be loving to others in a consistent and unfailing way. Enable me to be the kind of person people are attracted to because of Your love in me.

In Jesus' name I pray.

—*Stormie*

17

Purpose in My Imperfections

But I have raised you up for this very purpose,
that I might show you my power and that my
name might be proclaimed in all the earth.

EXODUS 9:16

Jesus, it's hard not to look in the mirror and see imperfections. Too many times all that I see is all that I wish I could change. Forgive me, Lord, for I know this is not only an insult to Your perfect and special design of me, but to Your plans of using me. You have raised me up, from the hair on my head to the tips of my toes, for a specific purpose. The very things that I wish I could change are not a mistake, but Your divine plan.

Lord, You even say that my imperfections and weaknesses are my *strength* (2 Corinthians 12:9). If this is so, then how beautiful it is to be imperfect! Though the world around me does everything to airbrush flaws, I stand firm knowing that I have the freedom in You to throw off pretenses and be *real*. Thank You that You have created me to fulfill a greater story than just my own. Use me, Lord, for Your glory.

In Jesus' name I pray.

—*Paige*

18

When I Feel Anxious

Do not be anxious about anything, but in every situation, by prayer and petition, with thanksgiving, present your requests to God. And the peace of God, which transcends all understanding, will guard your hearts and minds in Christ Jesus.

PHILIPPIANS 4:6-7

Lord, You have said in Your Word that we are not supposed to have anxiety about anything, but instead we are to *pray* about everything. Help me to do that. I get anxious about many things and I don't want to be that way. I know I can't live successfully if I am too often distracted by worry. Help me to tell You everything that is on my heart way before it gets out of control.

I lift up to You the things that cause me to feel anxious right now and thank You for the amazing peace You have promised in Your Word to those who pray— a peace that will guard my heart and mind. Thank You that You can help me overcome all anxiety so completely that I am no longer anxious about anything. Teach me to fully trust You in this.

In Jesus' name I pray.

—*Stormie*

19

Lord, Use Me to Change the World

Speak up for those who cannot speak for
themselves, for the rights of all who are destitute…
defend the rights of the poor and needy.

PROVERBS 31:8-9

Lord, I have a burning desire to impact this world. Thank You that though I am small, You are not, and Your presence in me is great enough to do *anything* You've called me to do. I long to leave a legacy that touches generations to come for Your Kingdom. My life is but a mist (James 4:14), yet through Your power, the things I give myself to can have an eternal impact. I am Your vessel.

Your Word says that You have put Your Spirit on me that I might bring justice to the nations (Isaiah 42:1). You have anointed me to preach good news to the poor, to bind up the brokenhearted, to proclaim freedom for the captives, to release those who've been imprisoned in darkness, and to give comfort for those who mourn (Isaiah 61:1-2). Father, I give my life to serve by Your side. Show me specifically who to reach, and help me to step out in faith. I'll follow You to the ends of the earth.

In Jesus' name I pray.

—*Paige*

20

Getting Close to God

Come near to God and he will come near to you.

JAMES 4:8

Lord, I want to be close to You and feel Your presence in my life. But I know that cannot happen if I don't spend time alone with You. Yet finding time alone to pray is sometimes difficult and I need Your help. Show me the things that draw me away from being with You and that are not necessary to my life. No one will ever know me as well or love me as much as You do. Only You can fill the places in me that feel empty or lonely.

Thank You, Lord, that when I draw near to You, You always draw near to me. I draw close to You right now and ask You to help me recognize the comfort of Your presence in my life. Help me to set aside time each day to be with You so that I can know You better and become more like You. I don't want a shallow relationship with You, Lord. I want it to be deep and life-changing.

In Jesus' name I pray.

—*Stormie*

21

Help Me Not to Compromise

The world and its desires pass away, but
whoever does the will of God lives forever.

1 John 2:17

Heavenly Father, there is so much compromise around me I fear I'm blurring lines that should be straight and clear. Reel me back in so I will feel Your instant tug when I am stepping too close to the edge. Give me clarity of vision in the areas of how I dress, how I present myself, how I talk, what I listen to and watch, and what I spend my time doing. Restore to me, especially, *Your* definition of purity.

Lord, I repent and ask You to reclaim my heart. Show me specifically what areas I'm compromising in and raise my standard to what is truly *Your* standard… not everyone else's. You have so much for me, Lord, and I don't want to miss out on it because I'm not fully giving myself to You. What benefit do I ever reap at the time from the things I'm now ashamed of (Romans 6:21)? May I never trade in Your precious treasures for the scum of this world.

In Jesus' name I pray.

—*Paige*

Sometimes It's Hard for Me to Pray

The eyes of the Lord are on the righteous and his ears are attentive to their prayer.

1 PETER 3:12

Lord, help me to remember that prayer is simply communicating with You, telling You what my concerns are and how I feel about my life and the way I feel about You. It's telling You what I want to see happen in my life and in the world around me. Often I feel like my life and thoughts are complicated and hard to express. But I know You understand me and my situation far better than I do.

Sometimes it's hard for me to pray because I'm not sure You will hear and answer. But Your Word says that You see me and my situation and that You are always open to my prayers and the things that concern me. I pray that the things *You* care about will be the things *I* care about as well. Help me to pray when I find it difficult and don't know what to pray. Help me believe that You always hear and answer.

In Jesus' name I pray.

—*Stormie*

23

I Escape to You

Come to me, all you who are weary and burdened, and I will give you rest.

MATTHEW 11:28

Lord Jesus, when You walked as a man on this earth, You often withdrew to a solitary place. After pouring Yourself out continually for others, it was in this lone getaway that You were renewed. Even as the Almighty Son of God, this is where You found Your strength. Lord, I escape to You now in this solitary place and moment, needing rest and renewal for my soul. I ask Your Spirit of peace to wash over me, rinsing away my stress, fears, and insecurity. Flood me with Your presence, that every pore in my body might exude Your glorious light.

Scripture says that when Moses came down the mountain from his private meeting with You he literally glowed. His face was so radiant that everyone knew he had just been in the midst of Your Almighty presence (Exodus 34:29-35). Lord, I humbly ask that You meet me here in this sacred moment. May Your presence leave me radiant and my heart utterly changed.

In Jesus' name I pray.

—*Paige*

24

When I Am Discouraged

Let us not become weary in doing good, for at the proper time we will reap a harvest if we do not give up.

GALATIANS 6:9

Lord, I thank You that You are the God of encouragement. When things happen in my life that are discouraging I know I will be encouraged whenever I read Your Word and sense Your peace and love for me. Help me to have far more faith in Your promises to me than I have in the opinions of others. Teach me to consistently reject any voice of discouragement because it is never from You. Enable me to be so familiar with Your voice to my heart that I immediately recognize a counterfeit.

Help me to not lose heart or grow weary of doing what is good and right in Your eyes. Keep me from becoming disheartened by circumstances *around* me and the things that happen *to* me. Help me instead to look forward to the good things I will reap in my life because I refused to let myself become weary while doing the right thing.

In Jesus' name I pray.

—*Stormie*

25

Reclaim What I've Lost

*I have loved you with an everlasting love…I will
build you up again, and you…will be rebuilt.*

JEREMIAH 31:3-4

Father, I come before You feeling broken in a thousand pieces. I've been slowly wandering away from You and I can't do this anymore. I've heard You call me, but I haven't wanted to listen. I've felt You whisper Truth, but I wanted You to be wrong. You knew how my decisions would end, yet I didn't want to be stopped. So now, here I am—at the end of myself. I need You. I refuse to take another step without You. I give You *everything*.

Your Word says that after my suffering You will restore me, make me strong, firm, and steadfast (1 Peter 5:10). You have promised to rebuild me, so Father, pour the foundation and lay the structures of my heart. When You created me, You knew the woman that You wanted me to be. Reclaim what I've lost and breathe Your life into my soul. Thank You, God, that as You restore me, You give me so much more than I could ever ask for or imagine (Ephesians 3:20). Lord, rebuild me.

In Jesus' name I pray.

—*Paige*

26

I Am Created for Good Things

We are God's handiwork, created in
Christ Jesus to do good works.

EPHESIANS 2:10

Dear Lord, I thank You for creating me and having a high purpose for my life. Help me to understand what that plan and purpose is. I don't want to waste time on things that will lead me away from the path You have for me. But I don't want to miss out on opportunities that will lead me toward what You want me to do. Open the doors You want me to go through. Close the doors that I should not enter. And give me the ability to tell the difference between the two.

Lord, I know that the best way for me to understand who I am is to better understand who *You* are. Help me to do that. Help me to read the Bible more so I can know You better. Help me to spend more time with You in prayer. Teach me to worship You every day, no matter what is happening, so I can stay on the path You have for me.

In Jesus' name I pray.

—*Stormie*

27

Lord, Guide My Choices

Whether you turn to the right or to the left, your ears will hear a voice behind you, saying, "This is the way; walk in it."

Isaiah 30:21

Lord Jesus, I come to You for direction. This is such a crucial time in my life, and I cling to Your guidance. Lord, the world offers all kinds of advice, but it's not their voice that I look to. I seek *Your plan* solely. Set my feet on the path that You have for me and illuminate the way. I lift every big decision weighing on me before Your throne. Lead me clearly that I might know exactly which way to go. Your Spirit is not one of confusion but of peace (1 Corinthians 14:33), so I know You will give me clarity.

I ask for a renewed sense of purpose in my smaller daily choices, knowing that how I spend each moment is how I live my life. Every choice matters. Remind me each morning as my feet touch the floor to commit my day to You. Father, I ask that Your Holy Spirit would be at my helm, guiding me through every choice, every day.

In Jesus' name I pray.

—Paige

28

Speaking Words That Please God

May these words of my mouth and this meditation of my heart be pleasing in your sight, LORD, my Rock and my Redeemer.

PSALM 19:14

Lord, help me to not think negative thoughts or say critical words about anyone. Forgive me for any time I have done that, for I know it does not please You. Help me to be careful about the words I speak so that I won't say anything that hurts someone. Help me to treat others with kindness, patience, and love. Enable me to build people up and not tear them down. I know that words matter and You have said in Your Word that "Those who guard their lips preserve their lives" (Proverbs 13:3).

Teach me to think before I speak so that I say words that are honest yet caring, sensitive and not cruel. I know that dishonest, insensitive, or mean thoughts and words show I have a serious heart problem. Even if someone says negative or critical words toward me, give me strength to not retaliate. Enable me to be more like You.

In Jesus' name I pray.

—*Stormie*

29

Being a Woman of Integrity

Charm is deceptive, and beauty is fleeting; but a woman who fears the LORD is to be praised.

PROVERBS 31:30

Heavenly Father, my culture's definition of a "true woman" is appalling. Please undo the damage that this has caused in me. Although the world likes to pretend that they value a woman's character, they only sell her sex appeal. I long to be a woman of integrity, for I know that is where *true* and *unfading* beauty lies. Help me to tune out the other voices screaming deception. Most of all, don't let me look to guys for my affirmation. My value and worth are sealed in You.

You've told us that man looks at the outward appearance but that You look at our heart (1 Samuel 16:7). Pour Your character inside me and teach me to walk with integrity. You've described a noble woman as being one who is passionate about her work, whose arms are open to the poor, who's clothed with strength and dignity, who speaks with wisdom and is not lazy (Proverbs 31:17-27). Lord, breathe these qualities into me as I pray. I stand in awe of You, Almighty God.

In Jesus' name I pray.

—*Paige*

30

Refusing Negative
Thoughts About Myself

The mouth speaks what the heart is full of.

MATTHEW 12:34

Lord, I pray that You would fill my heart abundantly with more of Your love, so that it flows into my thoughts and words. Help me to not think judgmental thoughts or say critical words about myself. I don't want to contradict who You say I am. You say I am valuable and have a purpose. You say You have made me to be Your daughter and You have a great future for me (Jeremiah 29:11-13). You say You will help me do what I need to do and You will bring everything You have promised to me to pass (Ephesians 1:13-14).

You say You will never leave me or forsake me. You say You will fill me with joy and hope by the power of Your Spirit (Romans 15:13). You say that if I stay focused on You, You will keep me in perfect peace. You have given me gifts, a calling, and a purpose. Enable me to speak words about myself that line up with what You say about me.

In Jesus' name I pray.

—*Stormie*

31

I Need a Reality Check

Why, you do not even know what will happen tomorrow. What is your life? You are a mist that appears for a little while and then vanishes.

JAMES 4:14

Heavenly Father, open my eyes. I feel as though I've been sleepwalking, and I can't afford to waste precious time. When I read Your Word I realize that I often devote myself to things that are fading away. Only what is unseen will last (2 Corinthians 4:18). Be my vision; rearrange my thoughts and priorities according to Your plan and what matters in eternity. You have given me an inheritance in heaven that will never perish, spoil, or fade (1 Peter 1:4), yet my time on earth is slipping away.

Help me to see my successes and troubles clearly, that I wouldn't base my life upon perishable things. I cannot depend on tomorrow, for that's not promised. I must follow You today. Lord, bind up the enemy who tries to control my thinking with the mindset of this world. What I do right now does matter and my life is precious. The reality that I see is not Your true reality. Remove the scales from my eyes. Awaken me.

In Jesus' name I pray.

—*Paige*

32

When Life Seems Overwhelming

From the ends of the earth I call to you, I call as my heart grows faint; lead me to the rock that is higher than I.

PSALM 61:2

Lord, sometimes I feel like my life is out of control and I am powerless to do anything about it. When my external circumstances and my internal emotions are more than I can handle, I feel I could explode. But I know You have the power to do anything—even change me and my circumstances. I thank You that even when what I am experiencing is too much for me, it is not too much for You. It is never beyond Your power to overcome.

Your Word says that when "the enemy pursues me… my spirit grows faint within me; my heart within me is dismayed" (Psalm 143:3-4). Help me to recognize the lies of the enemy when my life seems out of control so I can resist him. Teach me to keep focused on the truth of Your Word. You are the Rock that is higher than my circumstances and You are in control of my life.

In Jesus' name I pray.

—*Stormie*

33

You Are My Father

*I will be a Father to you, and you will be my
sons and daughters, says the Lord Almighty.*

2 Corinthians 6:18

Lord, thank You for being such a loving Daddy. It's amazing to me that You are our huge, all-powerful Creator of the Universe, yet You are also our sweet and adoring Father. I can't begin to wrap my mind around You. Where my own father has disappointed me, I pray that You would heal my heart and help me to forgive him. Your Word tells me that I am Your precious child. You call me Your beloved daughter who is worth far more than precious jewels (1 Thessalonians 1:4; Proverbs 31:10). You only want the best for me and promise to withhold no good thing (Psalm 84:11).

Lord, *You* are my Father. You're the Daddy I can count on, the strong arms that I'm safe in. At the end of the day, no earthly dad could ever compare to my perfect Heavenly Father, for there is no one higher than the King. You have crowned me as Your daughter, Your heir…Your princess. There is no greater honor than to be Your child. I love You, Father.

In Jesus' name I pray.

—*Paige*

34

When My Heart Is Distressed

Those who hope in the LORD will renew their strength. They will soar on wings like eagles; they will run and not grow weary, they will walk and not be faint.

ISAIAH 40:31

Lord, I come to You with a feeling of sadness in my heart and I ask You to take it away. Show me the burdens I am carrying that I should be bringing to You. I know that when I do, Your Word promises that "weeping may stay for the night, but rejoicing comes in the morning" (Psalm 30:5). I know that because I have come to You in the midst of my trouble You will save me out of my distresses (Psalm 107:13).

Thank You, Lord, that You have the power to take away all distress and enable me to always find joy in You. Help me run the race and not grow weary from carrying a weight my shoulders were not built to carry. Show me how to rise up in *Your* strength and not my own. Thank You that every day You are able to fill my heart with joy (Psalm 4:7).

In Jesus' name I pray.

—*Stormie*

35

Storing My Treasures in Heaven

For where your treasure is, there your heart will be also.

MATTHEW 6:21

Jesus, I pray that You'd help me to not get caught up in the material things around me. Don't let me spend so much of my time building up "stuff" rather than what will actually last. Your Word says to store up treasures in heaven where moth and rust do not destroy and where thieves do not break in and steal (Matthew 6:19). What *do* I treasure? Things of this earth or things of You? Everything I have here can and will be taken from me. Convict my spirit if I've allowed any idols in my life. Reveal to me anything that I've placed above You or that I wouldn't give up if You asked me to.

I lift up and commit my finances to You because every cent I have isn't mine, but Yours. How, specifically, do You desire for me to spend the money You've entrusted to me? Give me a heavenly perspective that I might be able to cut through the earthly "stuff" and put You in Your rightful place...*as Lord.*

In Jesus' name I pray.

—*Paige*

36

Taking Control of My Thoughts

Do not conform to the pattern of this world, but be transformed by the renewing of your mind.

ROMANS 12:2

Dear Lord, You have said in Your Word that we can "take captive every thought" (2 Corinthians 10:5). Help me do that. I don't want to have negative or bad thoughts, or thoughts that draw me into the world's way of thinking and away from Your ways. I want the renewed mind You have spoken of in Your Word. Help me to take charge of my thoughts and refuse to entertain those that do not please You or that lead me to be preoccupied with things that are outside of Your will for my life.

Help me to not entertain thoughts that run wild from one fear to the next or that cause anxiety in me. Enable me to reject thoughts that serve no good purpose and only take away from my life. Keep me from having thoughts that are scattered, and instead help me fill my mind with good things that bring peace and stability to my life.

In Jesus' name I pray.

—*Stormie*

37

I Feel Hopeless

The LORD your God is with you, the Mighty Warrior who saves. He will take great delight in you; in his love he will no longer rebuke you, but will rejoice over you with singing.

ZEPHANIAH 3:17

Lord, I'm plagued with hopelessness that's been holding me hostage for far too long. I've allowed my mind to drown in circumstances and sink into the pit of despair. Forgive me, Lord, for not reaching out for You sooner. You've been here all along with outstretched arms. Your Word says that though I am overwhelmed from every angle, I am not crushed…I am perplexed, but not in despair, I am persecuted, but not abandoned, struck down, but not destroyed (2 Corinthians 4:8-9).

Jesus, I claim Your name as the authority over my life and ask that You remove the hopelessness that has bound me and left me immobile. Greater is Your Spirit in me than anything else that tries to bring me down (1 John 4:4). You redeem my life from the pit and crown me with love and compassion (Psalm 103:4). I reach for the hand that was pierced so that I might be *saved* from this darkness…Jesus, don't let me waste this gift.

In Jesus' name I pray.

—*Paige*

38

Praising God No Matter What Happens

The people I formed for myself that
they may proclaim my praise.

ISAIAH 43:21

Lord, I know that I was created to worship You above all else. And You want me to trust You enough to worship You in all things—not in just the good times, but no matter what is happening in my life. I know that You are always worthy to be praised. So regardless of what is going on in and around me, I will worship You, for You are greater than anything I face.

I worship You as my Creator, my heavenly Father, and the Almighty, all powerful God for whom nothing is impossible. You are my redeemer, restorer, provider, and protector, and all Your ways are good. I praise You with my whole heart and thank You for Your unfailing love toward me (Psalm 9:1). I will not allow anything to keep me from worshipping You—not circumstances and not even someone else's bad behavior. I know when I worship You, I am doing Your perfect will and it is pleasing in Your sight.

In Jesus' name I pray.

—*Stormie*

39

Waiting for My Husband

*Take delight in the LORD and he will
give you the desires of your heart.*

PSALM 37:4

Lord, sometimes I get restless as I wait for my husband. It's so hard to hold out not knowing where or who he is. The enemy tries to confuse, disappoint, and discourage me constantly…making me doubt that You really *do* have a man for me. But Lord, I cling to Your Word which says that You withhold no good thing from those who walk uprightly with You (Psalm 84:11). You know the good desires of my heart because You've placed them in me. I trust in You and Your timing for their fulfillment.

People often say that my biblical standards for a man are too high, but I know that is Satan's scheme to tempt me to compromise. I have no expectations for a man other than the ones You've specifically told me to hold out for. Until I meet the beloved man that You have for me, help me to steer clear from the guys who are mere distractions. Lord, use this time to mold and shape me into the woman that You've created me to be.

In Jesus' name I pray.

—*Paige*

40

Moving into the Future God Has for Me

What no eye has seen, what no ear has heard, and what no human mind has conceived—the things God has prepared for those who love him.

1 CORINTHIANS 2:9

Dear Lord, You have said in Your Word that I cannot even imagine all You have waiting for me simply because I love You. And I know that the only way I can move into all that in the future is to walk closely with You every day. Help me to do that. I don't want to make plans without consulting You. I don't want to make up my own vision for my life and *expect* You to bless it. I want *You* to fulfill *Your* vision for my life.

I see in Your Word that the people who walked with You in their daily lives—like Abraham, Moses, and David—were the ones You blessed most and were called by You to do great things. Help me to be like that so I can do great things for You. Give me peace about my future because I have put it in Your hands.

In Jesus' name I pray.

—*Stormie*

41

Lord, Give Me Wisdom

Wisdom is sweet to your soul. If you find it, you will have a bright future, and your hopes will not be cut short.

PROVERBS 24:14 NLT

Heavenly Father, of all the things on my heart to ask of You, I come before You solely petitioning for wisdom. Lord, You know my circumstances. You know where I have been unwise in the past. I seek to truly honor You with my character, my choices, and my life. This is why I pray for an outpouring of Your wisdom. How am I to handle anything that comes my way without Your divine guidance and wise perspective? Father, I repent of my past foolishness. Forgive me for ever thinking that I knew better than You.

Your Word says that You give generously to *all who ask* without finding fault (James 1:5). Lord, I long for others to be transformed by Your radiant presence in me. Your wisdom is pure, peace-loving, considerate, submissive, full of mercy and good fruit, impartial, and sincere (James 3:17). Your wisdom is so beautiful—who wouldn't be drawn to that? May the wisdom You pour into me be a reflection of Your heart to those around me.

In Jesus' name I pray.

—*Paige*

42

How Do I See Answers to My Prayers?

We know that God does not listen to sinners. He listens to the godly person who does his will.

JOHN 9:31

Lord, You have said in Your Word that if we give You reverence by worshipping You and obeying Your laws, that You will hear our prayers. Help me to obey Your laws and live Your way. Where I have disobeyed You, I confess that before You and ask You to forgive me.

Lord, I worship You above all things. I reverence You for You mean more to me than anything else in my life. Help me to never think, speak, or act in any manner that is irreverent or apathetic toward You. I choose to live my life with gratitude to You without complaining, so that my worship is always pleasing in Your sight. Thank You for forgiving me when I come to You with a repentant heart. Enable me to live in a way that pleases You, so that You hear my prayers and answer them according to Your will for my life.

In Jesus' name I pray.

—*Stormie*

43

Forgiving Myself

Forget the former things; do not dwell on the past. See, I am doing a new thing! Now it springs up…I am making a way in the wilderness and streams in the wasteland.

ISAIAH 43:18-19

Jesus, I can't seem to let go of the mistakes that I've made. Every time I try to move forward, Satan throws my failures back in my face. Lord, You know that I have repented and surrendered to You with all of my heart. Your Word says that You have wiped my sins as far from me as the east is from the west (Psalm 103:12) and You have made my scarlet sins as white as snow (Isaiah 1:18).

Though the enemy would love to keep me in bondage, You have already lifted the chains off me— I've simply refused to accept Your freedom and forgive myself. Thank You, Lord, for Your incredible and unfailing mercy. I don't deserve it, but I receive it now wholeheartedly with joy and gratefulness in my heart. Today is a new day, a fresh start. You have set me free, so I am free indeed (John 8:36)!

In Jesus' name I pray.

—*Paige*

44

Establishing Right Priorities

"Love the Lord your God with all your heart and
with all your soul and with all your mind." This is
the first and great commandment. And the second
is like it: "Love your neighbor as yourself."

MATTHEW 22:37-39

Lord, my top priority in life is to love You with all my heart. And the next is to love others. Help me to do that. Loving You is easy, but sometimes loving others is not. But I know that when I get those priorities straight, the other priorities in my life will fall into place. Help me to put You first above all else. Help me to seek You first every day in prayer, in praise, and in Your Word.

Show me what the priorities in the rest of my life should be. Help me see clearly how I should divide up my time. I don't want to try to do so much that I don't do anything well, yet I don't want to neglect any part of what You want me to do either. Whatever I do, help me to honor You in it.

In Jesus' name I pray.

—*Stormie*

45

Lord, Reveal My Pride

Do nothing out of selfish ambition or vain conceit.

PHILIPPIANS 2:3

Lord, You've shown us in Your Word that if there's one sin that You hate, it's pride. Sometimes I overlook the pride in myself because I only think of the term as blatant arrogance. But Lord, I'm reminded how the most common and disguised pride is actually *insecurity*—the idea that I can't possibly reveal my problems or imperfections because I'm supposed to be perfect and everyone's looking at *me*. Father, forgive me for being so self-centered as to think the whole world even cares about my bad hair days or zits.

Scripture says I ought to be humble and value others above myself, not looking to my own interest but the interests of the others (Philippians 2:4). So much of my insecurity would disappear if I would only take my eyes off myself and focus on others. Life is not about me…it's about You, Lord. Reveal to me whatever form of pride has festered inside of me and wipe it out. Give me a humble spirit that reflects the attitude and glory of my Maker. You must become greater, and I must become less (John 3:30).

In Jesus' name I pray.

—*Paige*

When I Don't Feel Good About Myself

"For I know the plans I have for you," declares the LORD, "plans to prosper you and not to harm you, plans to give you hope and a future."

JEREMIAH 29:11

Dear Lord, sometimes I don't feel good about myself. I see myself with the critical eye of a judge and sentence myself to feeling inadequate. I know that is not the way You see me. You see me from the great future You have for me and not my past. I see all that You have done for me, but You see all that You *are* doing and *will* do in me.

Thank You that You see me as Your precious daughter, and every day You are making me to become more like You. When I am tempted to give in to negative thoughts about myself and my future, help me to resist the ploy of the enemy and refuse to go there. Keep me from giving in to self-focus, but rather lift my eyes to focus on You so I will praise You for everything that is good in my life.

In Jesus' name I pray.

—*Stormie*

Give Me Discernment

I am sending you out like sheep among wolves. Therefore be as shrewd as snakes and as innocent as doves.

MATTHEW 10:16

Father, each year that passes the more I see my desperate need for discernment. Too many times I've wandered down roads that seemed well lit and promised hope, only to later discover they were dingy, dark, and not what they promised. Lord, give me a discerning spirit that I might be able to sense when something is not right or of You. Most sin doesn't pose as evil, but rather as *good*. Keep my eyes wide open to this and my heart wise and shrewd. Help me to hide Your Word in my heart so that I might not sin against You (Psalm 119:11).

I am bombarded daily with so many messages from culture. I admit that at times I've been lazy and neglect to sort and discern *each one*. Don't let me buy into what the world feeds me; let me only be sustained by Your Truth. Give me the power through Your Spirit to test everything, hold on to good, and flee every kind of evil (1 Thessalonians 5:21-22). It's by Your standard that I live.

In Jesus' name I pray.

—Paige

Living with a Grateful Heart

*I will sacrifice a thank offering to you
and call on the name of the LORD.*

PSALM 116:17

Dear Jesus, I never thought of being thankful to You as a sacrifice until I read it in Your Word. But I see how it is a choice we make to acknowledge You and be thankful to You for all You have done for us. I also see that not everyone makes that choice—not even all of Your children. But I do make that choice right now to honor You and live with a grateful heart toward You every day.

I am beyond thankful for all You have done for me. You have saved me from death and You have given me a high purpose. You have protected me and given me Your Holy Spirit to lead, guide, and comfort me. I worship You for Who You are and praise You for all that You are doing and will do for me. No matter what is happening in my life, I call upon Your name with love, reverence, and thanksgiving in my heart.

In Jesus' name I pray.

—*Stormie*

Lord, Show Me My Spiritual Gifts

*Now you are the body of Christ, and
each one of you is a part of it.*

1 Corinthians 12:27

Lord, it delights me to know that Your Word says You have placed spiritual gifts inside each of Your children. I don't have to wander through life wondering why I'm here—You've given me a purpose and the tools to live it out. You've declared me a member in Your church, the Body of Christ, and have given me a specific part in it. Thank You that each of us has a different role, since, if we were all the same, where would the body be (1 Corinthians 12:19)?

Father, please show me the gifts that You have placed inside me. You have given me these gifts so I would use them, expand them, and freely give them. I desire to be a good steward with what You've entrusted to me; help me to use them as You've designed. How beautiful that not only do these gifts edify me and strengthen my relationship with You, but they are meant to bless others. Thank You, Lord, for gifting me with this incredible piece of Yourself.

In Jesus' name I pray.

—Paige

50

Choosing to Walk in the Spirit

You, however, are not in the realm of the flesh but are in the realm of the Spirit, if indeed the Spirit of God lives in you. And if anyone does not have the Spirit of Christ, they do not belong to Christ.

ROMANS 8:9

Dear Jesus, thank You that because I have received You as my Savior, I have Your Holy Spirit in me. Your Spirit in me is the sign that I am Yours now and I have the power to refuse to walk according to my fleshly desires. I am no longer controlled by my sinful nature. You have made the way, and I have chosen You, yet still I must make choices each day to walk in the Spirit and not allow myself to walk in the flesh.

Help me to choose every day to serve You and to walk Your way, being led by Your Holy Spirit in me. I know that those who walk in the flesh cannot please You, so help me to stand strong and set my mind on the things of the Spirit and refuse to be brought down into the preoccupations of the flesh (Romans 8:5).

In Jesus' name I pray.

—Stormie

51

Respecting Myself

*Like a gold ring in a pig's snout is a beautiful
woman who shows no discretion.*

PROVERBS 11:22

Heavenly Father, I fear I haven't been representing the dignity that You've given me. You have called me to be a woman of noble character who is respected. You have instructed me to present myself with beautiful modesty and a wise spirit. Lord, forgive me for trading in Your admirable qualities for worldly trends. My culture has glamorized provocative women with loose morals. I know You have higher standards for us because You cherish us more than we can understand.

You've placed Your beauty inside of me, that I wouldn't allow it to be slandered or trampled on. It breaks Your heart to see Your precious daughters throwing themselves at guys, accepting crude comments as compliments, and drawing inappropriate attention to their bodies. You created me for more than that, Lord. Remind me of my worth. Make my heart feel instantly sick the moment I present myself with less value than You've given me. You have crowned me as Your daughter and princess; You have inscribed Your royalty on my heart.

In Jesus' name I pray.

—*Paige*

52

Praying for Difficult People

Carry each other's burdens, and in this way
you will fulfill the law of Christ.

GALATIANS 6:2

Lord, I lift up to You the person in my life that I find most difficult to be around. I know You want me to love others the way that You love them, but I confess that in this case I find it very hard to do. I ask for a special infusion into my heart of Your love so that it overflows especially to the person who seems impossible to love. Show me what is going on in that person. Help me understand where he or she is troubled or hurt. Give me patience and understanding.

When someone becomes hard for me to deal with, enable me to remember to pray for them instead of becoming angry or resentful of them. Reveal to me anything in me that is contributing to the difficulties in this relationship. Show me a better way to relate to them that will bring good results. I pray that this challenging person will be touched by Your love and peace. Change the uncomfortable strain between us.

In Jesus' name I pray.

—*Stormie*

53

Give Me True Faith

If you have faith as small as a mustard seed, you can say to this mountain, "Move from here to there," and it will move. Nothing will be impossible for you.

MATTHEW 17:20

Lord Jesus, I ask for a greater measure of faith. I believe that You are the Creator of the universe and are all-powerful. Rid me of any doubt in my heart that would hinder Your work in me. You ask that I have faith to truly believe You are who You said, and You'll do what You've promised. I declare my trust in You.

Faith is being sure of what I hope for, and certain of what I cannot see (Hebrews 11:1). Give me a heart that is sure of Your Word and of Your Presence with me. Through prayer I am connected to the Source of Life! Lead me to ask in faith for the things that are in line with Your will, for it's then that You promise it will be given to me (Matthew 21:22). Lord, help me to pray with wholehearted faith, that my prayers would move mountains in my life and in others'.

In Jesus' name I pray.

—*Paige*

54

Not Letting Emotions Rule My Day

By your patience possess your souls.

LUKE 21:19 NKJV

Lord, I know You gave me the ability to feel emotions, but I also know that You don't want them to control or affect my life in a negative way. But sometimes when things don't go like I want them to it can feel like the end of the world. When I feel full of emotion, give me the strength to resist the negative ones by bringing every feeling to You. I know You understand them more than I ever can.

Help me to not live by my feelings because I know I am able to feel things that are wrong. I can *feel* ugly, or stupid, or like You don't care about me. But Your Word says that none of these things are true, and that I can't always trust my feelings to tell me the truth. Give me the ability to control my emotions and recognize the ones that have no validity. Teach me to express the ones that have a purpose. I want my emotions to be in Your control and ruled by Your truth.

In Jesus' name I pray.

—*Stormie*

55

Lord, Give Me Confidence

So do not throw away your confidence; it will be richly rewarded. You need to persevere so that when you have done the will of God, you will receive what he has promised.

HEBREWS 10:35-36

Father, if there's one thing I lack right now as I seek to follow Your calling, it's confidence. I feel so inadequate for the things You've set before me, but I know Your Word says You've given me everything I need for life and godliness (2 Peter 1:3). Lord, I think about Mary and how You told her the wildest news anyone could hear...*she was to have Your Son*. Yet her response was completely calm and sure: "May Your word to me be fulfilled" (Luke 1:38).

Jesus, I ask for that same faith. I ask for confidence—not in myself, but in You. I am Your vessel, God, and I believe that anything You choose to do through me will have incredible power. I repent of the ways that I've held You back because of my own doubt. I cast aside my selfishness and fear and declare that I can do *all* things through Christ who gives me strength (Philippians 4:13)!

In Jesus' name I pray.

—*Paige*

Rising Above Peer Pressure

You shall have no other gods before me.

EXODUS 20:3

Heavenly Father, I come to You and seek Your strength. Sometimes I feel pressure by certain people around me to do the things *they* are doing, even though it is not Your best for my life. Help me not to do anything that doesn't feel right in my soul, or that I know is wrong, or that does not glorify You. Enable me to get free of wanting to be liked by others more than wanting to please You. Help me to not feel like I have to fit in with *their* plans more than with *Your* plan. I want to look to You for approval and acceptance and not to others.

Rather than being influenced by others in a negative way, I pray that Your Spirit in me will draw others to You and influence *them* in a positive way. Enable *me* to be the influencer who leads others away from trouble. I want to live up to Your standard for my life and not someone else's. You are my God and my allegiance is to You.

In Jesus' name I pray.

—*Stormie*

Seeing Myself
Through God's Eyes

*For you created my inmost being; you knit
me together in my mother's womb.*

PSALM 139:13

Lord, give me Your eyes, because mine don't see clearly. When I look at myself, I see what I lack. When You look at me, You see Your cherished daughter for whom You've given everything. Father, thank You for creating me. Your Word says that I am fearfully and wonderfully made (Psalm 139:14). Help me to see that. When I look in the mirror, direct my eyes to specific parts of me and reveal the beauty in those areas that I've never noticed before. Show me a glimpse of why You created each part of me, that I might see myself the way You do.

Lord, thank You that when You look at me, You see the purpose and future that You have for me. You see the daughter You've redeemed, whose shame You've traded in for honor. Father, no one sees me as more beautiful or precious than You. You proved my worth when You sent Your only Son to die in my place. Because of Your sacrifice, the value of my life is beyond measure.

In Jesus' name I pray.

—Paige

When My Prayers Have Not Been Answered

Devote yourselves to prayer, being watchful and thankful.

COLOSSIANS 4:2

Lord, there are prayers that I have been praying for a while and I have not seen answers yet. Help me to do as You have said in Your Word and continue praying with a grateful heart. Thank You that You do hear my prayers. Help me to trust You to answer them in Your way and Your time. I know it is my job to pray and that You will answer as You see fit. Help me to do my job and pray according to Your will.

If You *are* answering my prayer and I have not recognized that because it wasn't answered the way I envisioned it, open my eyes to see the truth. If the answer is no, help me to rest in that because above all I want Your will to be done in my life. If I am to keep on praying about this, help me to press on and not lose heart while waiting for the answer You have for me.

In Jesus' name I pray.

—*Stormie*

Ignite My Passion

Whatever you do, work at it with all your heart…since you know that you will receive an inheritance from the Lord as a reward.

COLOSSIANS 3:23-24

Father, You've given me a purpose to live out in this world. Ignite a passion in my soul for the things You're calling me to do. Spark a fire in my heart for the specific people You've designed me to minister to. Let me overflow with compassion and love for them and be willing to serve them at all costs. Don't let me succumb to the lies of this world that tell me to only worry about myself and the best way to make money. I wholeheartedly give myself to Your fulfilling and radical plan for me. Don't let there be an apathetic bone in my body, for You've said that complacency will destroy (Proverbs 1:32).

Lord, I give You everything I love and everything I hate. Transform them both into passions that serve You. As Your follower, my life should be anything but dull and my heart should be nothing but passionate. May my life reveal to a dying world what an exhilarating and beautiful adventure it is to follow my Lord!

In Jesus' name I pray.

—*Paige*

60

Mending a Broken Heart

The righteous cry out, and the LORD hears them; he delivers
them from all their troubles. The LORD is close to the
brokenhearted, and saves those who are crushed in spirit.

PSALM 34:17-18

Lord, Your Word says that when I come to You with a humble heart You hear my prayers and save me from my problems. I come to You now with a heart that hurts. I feel like my heart is broken, either from things that have happened in the past or from something that is happening right now. I pray that You would mend and heal it. Take the pain away and help me to cope with the situation that has caused it.

Thank You that You promise to hear my prayers and deliver me out of trouble. You are near to those who have a broken heart, and I need the presence of Your Holy Spirit to bring comfort to my heart now. Give me a heart that is free of pain and filled with certainty of the good days You have ahead for me.

In Jesus' name I pray.

—*Stormie*

Lord, Help Me Be Pure

*But among you there must not be even a hint of
sexual immorality, or of any kind of impurity…
because these are improper for God's holy people.*

EPHESIANS 5:3

Jesus, I come to You and plead for my purity. It is
so hard to be pure not only physically, but in my mind
and heart. Strengthen me against the fleshly desires that
war in my soul. I surrender to You and ask that You
would fill me with what is right, pure, lovely, and admi-
rable (Philippians 4:8). It is only by Your grace that I
can stand firm in the midst of temptation.

Lord, show me specifically what it means to walk
out purity according to Your standards, and convict me
if I'm disobeying them. Thank You, Father, that You're
not keeping me from goodness and pleasure, but rather
protecting me from harm so I can fully enjoy sex as You
intended. Create in me a pure heart, O God, and renew
an unwavering spirit in me (Psalm 51:10). Wipe away
all my past mistakes that I may be pure and whole in
Your sight. I'm so grateful for Your grace, and I cling to
Your protection.

In Jesus' name I pray.

—*Paige*

62

Staying Free of Envy

A heart at peace gives life to the body, but envy rots the bones.
PROVERBS 14:30

Dear Lord, help me to never compare myself and my circumstances to others. I don't want to feel envious of anyone, for I know that nothing good comes out of that. It only brings confusion and evil into my life (James 3:16). Help me to not think about what someone else has that I don't. Help me, instead, to think about all that *You* have for me—Your love, Your gifts, Your help, Your power, and Your provision for me.

I know that envy only creates misery in the person who has it. So if there is ever someone who is envious of me for any reason, I pray that Your love in me would be so strong that it would overshadow any negative feelings in that person. When I recognize envy in someone toward me, remind me to pray for that person to be free of that terrible and destructive attitude. Enable me to be completely free of the rottenness of envy in my life.

In Jesus' name I pray.

—*Stormie*

63

Lord, I Need Healing

LORD my God, I called to you for help, and you healed me.
PSALM 30:2

Jesus, I come before You, knowing You are the Ultimate Healer. My body is stricken with (pain/illness) and I look to You first and foremost for restoration. You knit my body together and know every ounce of it (Psalm 139:13). There is no one who knows what's going on inside of me better, and there is no one with greater power to heal me. Lord, *in Jesus' name*, I ask that You would heal my (area of pain or disease) and restore me completely back to health. I pray that You release any hold that the enemy has over me and wash me in Your cleansing blood.

Father, pour out Your Holy Spirit on me that my body would be filled not with the weakness of flesh but with Your powerful Presence. I believe that not only are You able to heal me, but that You desire to use my life for Your amazing purpose. I trust You in *all* things, and know that it is by Your wounds that I have received ultimate healing (Isaiah 53:5).

In Jesus' mighty name I pray.

—*Paige*

64

I Don't Want to Live in Fear

There is no fear in love; but perfect love casts out fear, because fear involves torment. But he who fears has not been made perfect in love.

1 John 4:18 nkjv

Lord, I know You don't want me to live in fear, because fear doesn't come from You. You want me to trust You instead. When I see things that are happening in the world it makes me afraid of what could happen to me or the people close to me. Too often I am afraid of what people think, and I know that "The fear of man brings a snare, but whoever trusts in the Lord shall be safe" (Proverbs 29:25 nkjv).

Thank You that Your perfect love casts out all fear. I open my heart and ask for a fresh flow of Your perfect love in me. Help me to stay close to You so I can always feel Your love flowing through me and erasing all fear (2 Timothy 1:7). Keep me protected and away from every frightening threat. I know that the closer I am to You, the farther fear is from me.

In Jesus' name I pray.

—*Stormie*

65

What Is True Love?

And now these three remain: faith, hope and love. But the greatest of these is love.

1 Corinthians 13:13

Father, I feel like my definition of love has been tainted. Everywhere I turn people talk about being "in love," yet it doesn't even come close to the love that You've defined. Lord, I don't want to give away the words "I love you" loosely. I realize that they are not just some romantic feeling but actually a commitment when I say them. Your Word says that love is patient and kind. That it does not envy or boast, and it isn't proud. It is never rude, self-seeking, or easily angered, and it keeps no record of wrongs. You said love does not delight in evil but rejoices with the truth. It always protects, always trusts, always hopes, and always perseveres. Above all, love never fails (1 Corinthians 13:4-8).

Lord, as the Author of love, I ask that You would write this definition on my heart that its truth might lead me. Protect me from jading the purity of true love by succumbing to the world's idea of it. I bask in Your love for me and ask that it may overflow.

In Jesus' name I pray.

—*Paige*

66

Understanding My Purpose

*May He grant you according to your heart's
desire, and fulfill all your purpose.*

PSALM 20:4 NKJV

Dear Lord, thank You that You created me for a purpose. Thank You that You have saved me and called me with a holy calling according to the purpose You have for my life (2 Timothy 2:9). I ask for the wisdom and knowledge I need to understand what my calling is (Ephesians 1:17-18). I know that I will never find true happiness and peace until I am doing what You have called me to do. Even if I don't know all the details, enable me to sense the direction in which I should be going—as well as the direction in which I should clearly *not* be going.

I know that I am called to serve You and serve others, so I ask You to show me how to do that. Reveal to me the gifts and talents You have put in me so that I can serve Your purposes best. Give me a clear vision for my life. I don't want to strive to be something that You have not created or called me to be.

In Jesus' name I pray.

—*Stormie*

Teach Me to Make Disciples

Therefore go and make disciples of all nations,
baptizing them in the name of the Father
and of the Son and of the Holy Spirit.

MATTHEW 28:19

Lord, Your Word says to make disciples of all nations, but sometimes I don't even know where to start. Show me how to build strong relationships with people and invest in their lives. Help me to be more aware of people's needs. Sometimes they're obvious, but other times they're not. I rely on Your guidance to show me who to serve and how to minister to each person. Give me gracious boldness in order to share about You with others.

Jesus, when You walked among us, You tangibly cared for people before You ministered to them. Though You knew their ultimate spiritual need, You always met their physical needs too. This proved Your truth and love to them. Father, equip me to be a compassionate leader and example. Make my heart's desire to spend time pressing into You and Your Word. Pour into me, that I might learn from You how to pour into others.

In Jesus' name I pray.

—Paige

68

Bearing Good Fruit

The fruit of the Spirit is love, joy, peace, forbearance,
kindness, goodness, faithfulness, gentleness and self-control.
GALATIANS 5:22-23

Heavenly Father, I know that You are the God of all creativity and fruitfulness. I ask You to plant the seeds of creativity and fruitfulness in me so that I can bear good fruit in my life. Help me to "be like a tree planted by the rivers of water, that brings forth its fruit in its season" so that I can prosper in everything I do (Psalm 1:3 NKJV). Enable me to have a fruitful life that is full of good things.

Thank You that the Holy Spirit in me produces the fruit of Your Spirit. I pray that You would grow in me Your love, joy, and peace. Help me to increase in patience, kindness, and goodness. Enable me to exhibit great faithfulness, gentleness, and self-control so that I reflect Your nature. I know that I can only produce that kind of fruit in my life because Your Spirit is in me. I pray that these virtues will become visible in me as a sign to others that You are working powerfully in my life.

In Jesus' name I pray.

—*Stormie*

69

Promises in My Pain

*And we know that all things work together
for good to those who love God, to those who
are called according to His purpose.*

ROMANS 8:28 NKJV

Father, I can't see what You're doing right now. All
I see and feel is this pain that I'm going through. Open
my eyes, Lord. Your Word says You are good, You'll
never leave me, and that I have every reason to trust
You. Scripture says that You are the Father of compassion and the God of all comfort, who comforts us in our
troubles so we can then console others (2 Corinthians
1:3-4). You not only see us through our trials, but use
them to encourage and minister to others.

Your ways are not mine…*they are better*. Thank You
that nothing I go through is wasted because You always
have a purpose through my pain. What Satan planned
to be my demise, You planned to showcase redemption's story. Lord, I trust and submit to You in whatever
You're doing. Exchange my sorrow for gladness and my
nearsighted eyes for eternal hope. I cling to Your promises, for they promise to bring good.

In Jesus' name I pray.

—*Paige*

Resisting Temptation

The Lord knows how to deliver the godly out of temptations.

2 PETER 2:9 NKJV

Lord, I know that You never lead us *into* temptation, but You will always lead us *away* from it when we ask You (James 1:13). So whenever I am tempted to get off the path You have for me, I pray that You will strike my conscience and give me strength to stand strong against it. Help me to resist anything that entices me away from Your best for my life.

I know that no one is hidden from Your sight and that You see all things (Hebrews 4:13). I want everything I do to be approved by You. Make me aware at all times of what is happening around me so that I am not taken by surprise. Keep me from being attracted to someone or something that is not good for my life. Save me from my own weaknesses. Where I have fallen into temptation already, I pray You would strengthen me to stand strong and resist that plan of the enemy for my life.

In Jesus' name I pray.

—*Stormie*

71

I Am Your Ambassador

*We are therefore Christ's ambassadors, as though
God were making his appeal through us.*

2 CORINTHIANS 5:20

Lord, thank You that You have entrusted me as Your ambassador. What an honor that You allow my name to be associated with Yours. I don't take this lightly and I cling to You, asking for Your Spirit to lead me. I understand the seriousness of the fact that if I claim to follow You, *I actually need to.* There are too many hypocrites and fakes out there and I don't want to be one of them. They leave an unbelieving world confused about You because their lives don't show evidence of Your love, grace, and power.

Help me to be a true witness who has given my life to You and therefore can only live as You lead me. You tell us to be wise in the way that we act towards outsiders (Colossians 4:5) because we may be the only evidence of You that they're aware of. Lord, be the difference in me that others can't ignore. I long for unbelievers to wonder and ask what beautiful thing I have that they don't…so I can simply say, *Jesus.*

In Your name I pray.

—Paige

Refusing to Be Desperate

Be alert and of sober mind. Your enemy the devil prowls around like a roaring lion looking for someone to devour.

1 PETER 5:8

Dear Lord, help me to be on guard against the many bad influences around me in this world. Enable me to stand strong in resisting them. I don't want to be weak and so desperate to fit in with a certain group or a certain person that I will do something or watch something that I know is not right or good for my life. Help me to be aware and not naïve about the dangers. Teach me to recognize a situation that has the potential to be bad.

I know You have called me to purity and holiness. Keep me from ever compromising on that. Where I have already compromised and have seen, watched, or done something that is not pleasing to You, I ask You to forgive me and enable me to resist any desperation to succumb to the pressure of the ungodly. I want to be desperate only for more of You and all You have for me.

In Jesus' name I pray.

—*Stormie*

73

Lord, Guard My Heart

*Guard your heart above all else, for it
determines the course of your life.*

PROVERBS 4:23 NLT

Heavenly Father, I feel a war raging for my heart. Everyday I'm lured and seduced by something new that seeks to steal all that You've given me. Jesus, I hide my heart in Your hands, knowing it's the only safe place. Protect and preserve it so that I might not be hardened or jaded by this world. Show me how to have integrity in my relationships so that I wouldn't tear down the walls that were meant to be boundaries.

Lord, keep the key to my heart tightly in Your hands. I look to *You* to decide when and to whom to give it away. Your Word says not to arouse or awaken love until it so desires (Song of Songs 2:7), and I know only You have the authority over that timing. Guard my heart so that no one would come and steal its precious inmost pieces—and most of all, help me not to carelessly give them away. Remind me of my worth. Seal me with Your love, truth, and value.

In Jesus' name I pray.

—*Paige*

Making Wise Decisions

*If any of you lacks wisdom, you should ask
God, who gives generously to all without
finding fault, and it will be given to you.*

JAMES 1:5

Dear Lord, I pray that You will give me wisdom so I can always make good choices. Help me to seek Your wisdom in all things and to pay attention to the advice of wise people. Lead me away from counsel that is not wise or not godly. Help me to grow in wisdom and understanding every time I read Your Word (Proverbs 4:5-6).

Thank You that wise decisions can protect me from evil (Proverbs 2:10-12), save me from danger (Proverbs 3:23), and help me to have a long life (Proverbs 3:16). I know that to fear and reverence You is the beginning of all wisdom (Proverbs 9:10). Help me to do that without fail every day. Teach me to value wisdom, for Your Word says it is greater than having riches (Proverbs 16:16). Remind me to always inquire of You before I make any decision. Help me to grow in wisdom so that I make the best decisions every day.

In Jesus' name I pray.

—*Stormie*

Take Away My Anger

*A gentle answer turns away wrath, but
a harsh word stirs up anger.*

PROVERBS 15:1

Dear Jesus, I confess to You that I have anger stored up inside of me. I don't know exactly how it got there, but I hate the way that it flames up as a hot temper. Lord, I don't want to be that kind of person. It's not fair to those around me, and it's certainly not a quality that You want me to have. Your Word says to rid myself of anger, rage, malice, slander, and anything like it (Colossians 3:8). Instead, as Your dearly loved child, You've called me to clothe myself with compassion, kindness, gentleness, and patience (Colossians 3:12).

Father, I ask for a fresh outpouring of these specific qualities. In Your name, rip out the anger that has dug its roots into my heart. Show me specifically what is at the core of my temper and, if I am holding unforgiveness in my heart against someone, reveal it to me. Deliver me from this bondage that I might be able to love more freely and abundantly. Help me to seek Your peace and be a woman of patience in every situation.

In Jesus' name I pray.

—Paige

Staying Strong in Difficult Times

Be on your guard; stand firm in the
faith; be courageous; be strong.

1 Corinthians 16:13

Dear Lord, I thank You that You have given me Your Holy Spirit to be my Comforter and Helper. I am especially grateful for that in the tough times of my life. I know that hard things happen to everyone at one time or another, but You are always there for those who turn to You. I turn to You now and ask You to bring good out of the things that are happening or have happened that trouble me or bring me pain. Help me to be watchful in prayer, strong in faith, courageous, and unafraid.

Thank You that You care about the things I care about and that You understand my struggles even better than *I* do. Enable me to not only stay strong when I go through difficult situations, but to grow even stronger because I have put my hope in You and depend on You to bring me through it successfully. Teach me to always be watchful in prayer and growing stronger in faith.

In Jesus' name I pray.

—*Stormie*

Keep My Eyes on You

I keep my eyes always on the LORD. With him
at my right hand, I will not be shaken.

PSALM 16:8

Lord Jesus, sometimes everything feels like such a mess around me. Yet I find that when my world is spinning, it's only because I've taken my eyes off of You. Not only are You the Creator of Heaven and Earth, but in You, *all things hold together* (Colossians 1:17). Lord, be my center. Keep my eyes fixed and focused on You so that no matter what crashes around me, I can never fall apart.

Help me not to gaze too long at the things of this world so that my eyes wouldn't drift from You. God, You are my Rock and my Foundation. You are the gravity that keeps my feet on the ground. When my eyes are on You, everything else comes into proper focus. It's as though You become the glasses through which I see the world. Lord, Your ways bring me joy and Your vision brings me peace. I keep my sight ever on my Precious King.

In Jesus' name I pray.

—*Paige*

I'm Concerned About My Safety

If you say, "The LORD is my refuge," and you make the Most High your dwelling, no harm will overtake you, no disaster will come near your tent.

PSALM 91:9-10

Dear Lord, the world can seem like such a dangerous place and sometimes I fear for my safety. I pray that You would protect me from the plans of evil people and keep me from danger, accidents, or diseases. I pray also for my family members and friends, that You would keep them safe and protected too.

Thank You that You have given Your angels charge over me to keep me in all my ways (Psalm 91:11). I know that I cannot do whatever I want and expect You to protect me from the consequences of those choices. So I ask You to guide me. Help me to hear the voice of Your Holy Spirit speaking to my heart at all times, telling me the way I should go and what I should do or not do. Show me how to keep the noise of my life down so I can hear You leading me.

In Jesus' name I pray.

—*Stormie*

Help Me to Be a Listener

When there are many words, sin is unavoidable,
but the one who controls his lips is wise.

PROVERBS 10:19 HCSB

Lord, I've been noticing for some time now that there are very few people who listen more than they talk. It's always hurtful when I spend an hour with a friend and they hardly stop once in their sharing to ask how I am. Lord, I know that is not a characteristic of You and I pray that if there's any glimpse of that in me You would pull it out from the roots. I long to be a good listener, Father—someone who demonstrates genuine concern for others far beyond their concern for themselves (Philippians 2:3).

Please forgive me for the times I've been selfish. Keep my heart in its rightful place. Help me not only to be a better listener with others, God, but with You. Too often I throw my problems at You and walk away… not patiently quieting myself to hear from You. Your Voice is all that matters, so Lord, right now I quiet my soul and come before You just to listen. Thank You for caring enough to listen to me.

In Jesus' name I pray.

—Paige

Purify My Thoughts

Finally, brothers and sisters, whatever is true, whatever is noble, whatever is right, whatever is pure, whatever is lovely, whatever is admirable—if anything is excellent or praiseworthy—think about such things.

Philippians 4:8

Dear Lord, help me to think about things that are true, honest, and faith-filled, and not false, deceitful, or full of doubt. Teach me to have thoughts that are honorable, admirable, and superior, and never thoughts that are mean, low-minded, or dishonorable. Enable me to think about whatever is fair, right, or proper, and never unlawful, unfair, or biased.

Help me to entertain thoughts that are pure and untainted by evil, and never any that are corrupted or unholy. Enable me to have thoughts about whatever is lovely and pleasing, and refuse thoughts about anything ugly or offensive. Help me to dwell on what is positive and not negative, moral and not immoral, excellent and not low-minded. I want to think about things that are valuable, commendable, and uplifting, and not anything that is worthless, disparaging, or depressing. Help me to think thoughts that please You.

In Jesus' name I pray.

—*Stormie*

81

I Don't Feel Adequate to Your Call

For I am the LORD your God, who takes hold of your right hand and says to you, Do not fear; I will help you.

ISAIAH 41:13

Lord, the things You're calling me to do are so big that at times I can't help but feel overwhelmed. I want to do whatever You ask, but Lord, I'm afraid. I don't feel adequate or worthy of the opportunities You've set before me. I know Your Word says if anyone serves, he should do it with the strength *You* provide (1 Peter 4:11), so I cling to Your provision. Father, it's only through You that I am qualified.

Pour Your peace and confidence into me that I might cast fear aside and step into the plan that You have for me. Give me vision for Your purpose so that I wouldn't miss the point by merely thinking of myself. Lord, do Your will in my life and don't ever let me stand in Your way. I count on You for the words, the strength, the ability, and the wisdom to do whatever You ask. I trust that if You call me to do something, it's *only* because You'll equip me.

In Jesus' name I pray.

—*Paige*

Faith to Believe for the Impossible

Everything is possible for one who believes.

MARK 9:23

Dear Lord, I am grateful that You can take the smallest amount of faith and grow it into faith that can move mountains (Matthew 17:20). Your Word says that You have already given us some faith (Romans 12:3), but I need Your help to step out and act on the faith I have in order for it to grow. You have said in Your Word that it is impossible to please You if we don't have faith (Hebrews 11:6). I want to please You so I confess any doubt in me about You or Your Word as sin.

Your Word says, "According to your faith let it be done to you" (Matthew 9:29). That is very scary because there are some impossible situations in my life and I don't see how they can be overcome. And I don't want my lack of faith to limit what You want to do in each case. But You are the God for whom nothing is impossible. I believe You can do the impossible in my life.

In Jesus' name I pray.

—*Stormie*

83

Show Me How to Use My Life

Wake up, sleeper…Be very careful, then, how you
live—not as unwise but as wise, making the most
of every opportunity, because the days are evil.

EPHESIANS 5:14-16

Lord, You have said my life is but a breath and that my days are like a fleeting shadow (Psalm 144:4). I take this deeply to heart, and surrender to You my every moment. Don't let me waste a precious second that You've given me. Holy Spirit, lead me clearly so that I will follow Your will. Show me the specific things that You're calling me to pursue and raise up Your purpose in me.

Father, I know You have placed me here for such a time as this (Esther 4:14). The needs and darkness are great, but Your power and light are greater. I long to serve You and Your beloved people. Help me to make the most of every opportunity with everyone I encounter, that they might not walk away without experiencing You. Awaken my soul to understand why I'm here and what You've called me to do for the days You've given me. My life is *Yours*.

In Jesus' name I pray.

—*Paige*

The Hardest Thing About Prayer

You do not have because you do not ask.

JAMES 4:2

Dear Lord, the hardest thing about prayer is not knowing when You will answer my prayers or wondering if You will. Help me to have faith that You hear my prayers and will answer them in Your way and in Your time. Help me to recognize the answers to my prayers even when they don't turn out like I thought they would be answered.

Sometimes it feels like there is too much to pray about and the issues are so big that I don't even know where to start. Help me to remember that prayer is simply communicating with You about what is in my heart. And Your Word says the Holy Spirit in us helps us pray (Romans 8:26). I ask You, Holy Spirit, to help me pray. Even when I find it hard to pray out loud in front of other people, help me to focus more on You than on myself or whoever is listening. Teach me to pray in power.

In Jesus' name I pray.

—*Stormie*

Purify My Mind, Mouth, and Heart

Those who consider themselves religious and yet do not keep a tight rein on their tongues deceive themselves, and their religion is worthless.

JAMES 1:26

Heavenly Father, purify me. My thoughts, words, and motives need a deep cleaning. Wash away any filthy language, impure thoughts, and selfish intentions that have been festering in me. Lord, don't let any unwholesome talk come from my mouth, but only what is helpful for building others up according to their needs (Ephesians 4:29). Forgive me for grieving Your Spirit when I use my words carelessly and harbor sin in my heart.

Lay a boundary line in me that I might not cross with things like gossip, dirty language, and coarse jokes. Scripture calls our tongue a fire that can corrupt the whole person (James 3:6) and says that our words have the power to bring life or death (Proverbs 18:21). Lord, may the words of my mouth and the meditation of my heart bring *life* and be pleasing in Your sight (Psalm 19:14). Purify me from the inside out, that my conscience would always be clear before You.

In Jesus' name I pray.

—*Paige*

Refusing to Feel Worthless

Therefore, there is now no condemnation
for those who are in Christ Jesus.

ROMANS 8:1

Lord, sometimes I feel a sense of worthlessness—as if I am not worthy to receive Your blessings. Sometimes I have hesitated to pray because I don't feel I am worthy to receive answers to my prayers. Help me to remember that if I have violated Your laws or done something that is not pleasing in Your sight or glorifying to You, I must confess it before You and repent of it so that the air between us will be clear.

Help me to remember that it is because of Jesus that I am seen as righteous before You. When You look at me You see *His* goodness. So no matter who makes me feel badly, those feelings never come from You. Help me to recognize that only the enemy, cruel people, or my own thoughts can make me feel worthless. Enable me to refuse to live with feelings of low worth when You—and all Jesus did on the cross for me—have made me worthy.

In Jesus' name I pray.

—*Stormie*

Help Me Not to Judge Others

Do not judge, or you too will be judged. For in the same way you judge others, you will be judged.

MATTHEW 7:1-2

Lord, help me not to be a judgmental person. I know the damage that this can cause and I don't want any part of it. Your Word says there is only one Lawgiver and Judge—the one who is able to save and destroy… and that is *You* (James 4:12). Lord, forgive me for the times that I have looked at someone condemningly. I have no right to do that. Help me to separate my own experiences from how I think everyone else should be operating. You have laid out Truth in Scripture that lays the foundation for our lives. But Your Spirit leads each of us in a special, personal, and specific way…and Your leading will look slightly different in each of Your children.

You call us to discern and identify the fruit in a believer, but never to judge them. Help me to know the difference. Thank You so much for the unbelievable grace that You have given me. May I always pour out the mercy that You have extended to me.

In Jesus' name I pray.

—*Paige*

Finding God's Will for My Life

Not everyone who says to me, "Lord, Lord," will enter the kingdom of heaven, but only the one who does the will of my Father who is in heaven.

MATTHEW 7:21

Dear Lord, I know from Your Word that only those who do Your will live forever (1 John 2:17). And You don't want me to live for just myself, but to do Your will (1 Peter 4:2). *Your* will is far more important to me than my own, so reveal to me Your perfect will for my life. Guide my every step until I am in the center of it.

I confess to You the things I have done that I know are *not* Your will for my life. Forgive me and help me to never do anything outside of Your will again. If I am doing something now that is not Your perfect will for me and I am not recognizing that, show me so I can confess it before You and correct it. "I delight to do Your will, my God; your law is within my heart" (Psalm 40:8). I pray Your Word will guide me in everything I do.

In Jesus' name I pray.

—*Stormie*

I'm Here for a Reason

The God who made the world and everything in it…is not served by human hands, as if he needed anything. Rather, he himself gives everyone life and breath and everything else…God did this so that they would seek him and perhaps reach out for him and find him, though he is not far from any one of us.

ACTS 17:24-27

Lord, I know You don't *need* me. I know You have the power to do everything You're calling me to do Yourself—and a million times better. The fact that You still *choose* to have me work alongside You and live out this purpose You've breathed into my soul is humbling. You knew me before I was born. You knew all of my faults and failures, yet You still chose to put me on this earth.

I know that I am here in this exact point in time for a reason, and I rest in Your purpose for my life. When I feel alone, it's not because You've left me. Father, You are never far, so I seek You and reach out for Your hand.

In Jesus' name I pray.

—*Paige*

Seeing My Body as Precious

*Don't you know that you yourselves are God's temple
and that God's Spirit dwells in your midst?*

1 Corinthians 3:16

Dear Lord, I know my body is precious because You created it and it is where Your Holy Spirit resides. Help me to take care of it the way You want me to. I give my body to You as a living sacrifice and ask You to help me appreciate it and treat it in a way that is pleasing to You (Romans 12:1). Help me to not be critical of it but to be thankful for all that it does and can do.

I submit to You my habits of eating and exercising. Break down any bad habits I have and set me free to do what's right. Teach me the right way to care for my body. You have made it to function in an amazing way, so help me to stop doing anything that interferes with that process. Give me knowledge and self-control and help me to choose life in every decision I make with regard to my body, remembering always that it belongs to You.

In Jesus' name I pray.

—*Stormie*

Lord, You Are Unchanging

Jesus Christ is the same yesterday and today and forever.
HEBREWS 13:8

Lord, in a world where everything is always changing, thank You for being constant. In a culture where people's opinions change faster than the wind, thank You that Your Word remains the same. I don't have to be tossed around from the breaking news to the latest trends. Lord, forgive me for rebelling against Your Truth just because my culture has mistaken what You call evil for "normal" and "good." Your Word says to ask for the ancient paths, the good way, and walk in it (Jeremiah 6:16). My feet are solid only on Your timeless path.

You are the same God who parted the Red Sea and breathed the universe into existence, and yet You're here listening to me and working with the exact same power in my life. Remind me to *believe!* Time is stretched out like a horizon before You with no beginning and no end. Give me eyes that see from Your eternal perspective, that I might live wisely while I walk on this ground.

In Jesus' name I pray.

—*Paige*

Guide Me in the Right Direction

Wait on the LORD; be of good courage, and He shall strengthen your heart; wait, I say, on the LORD!

PSALM 27:14 NKJV

Dear Lord, I am grateful that You speak to the hearts of those who love You and You bless all those who live Your way (Isaiah 30:18). Thank You that when I call on You, You hear my prayers and answer (Isaiah 30:19). The deep cry of my heart today is that I will always stay on the correct path. I want to be in the right place at the right time in order to move into all You have for me.

Lead me, Holy Spirit, in the way I should go every day. Help me to wait patiently on You, Lord, for direction. I don't want to rush off on my own without any clear leading. I don't want to delay the process of becoming who You made me to be by taking a wrong turn. I wait on You now, knowing You will strengthen my heart and my faith to stand strong in courage.

In Jesus' name I pray.

—*Stormie*

Strengthen My Heart Against Temptation

Watch and pray so that you will not fall into temptation. The spirit is willing, but the flesh is weak.

MATTHEW 26:41

Father, too many times I've waited until I am in the midst of strong temptation to pray for Your help. Even though You are so good to always provide a way out and give me strength when I call on You (1 Corinthians 10:13), sometimes in the heat of the moment I've chosen not to listen and walked right into the sin. If I had only built myself up in prayer ahead of time against that temptation, I could have avoided it all together.

Lord, You and I know exactly where I am weakest. I lift these areas up to You right now and pray in advance that You would give me victory over temptation. Grant me discernment in all situations so that I will not walk right into a snare. Help me to listen to Your voice when it warns me, and not cast it aside. Your Spirit is so gracious to speak to my conscience and give me all of the help that I need. I put on Your armor and depend on Your shield.

In Jesus' name I pray.

—*Paige*

Choosing a New Beginning

*Therefore, if anyone is in Christ, he is a
new creation; old things have passed away;
behold, all things have become new.*

2 CORINTHIANS 5:17 NKJV

Lord Jesus, I believe You are the Son of God, and
no one comes to the Father except through You (John
14:6). I thank You that You laid down Your life on a
cross for me and then rose from the dead to prove You
are God and to save me from death and hell (Romans
10:9). I receive You as my Savior. I confess my sins and
failings before You and ask You to forgive me for them
all so that I can be cleansed (1 John 1:9). Thank You that
I can spend eternity with You and have a better life now.

Thank You that You have made it possible for me
to have a new beginning. Because I have received You,
I am now a new creation. Thank You for giving me
Your Holy Spirit to dwell in me (Romans 8:9). Teach
me how to live like the new creation You have made
me to be.

In Jesus' name I pray.

—*Stormie*

95

Show Me My Purpose

Where there is no vision, the people perish.
PROVERBS 29:18 KJV

Lord, I come before You humbled. You are the Creator of the universe who decides whether or not I take another breath…and yet You keep me breathing. This alone is proof that I'm here for a reason. From the beginning of time, You knew me and had a purpose for my life. You've said in Your Word that the greatest thing we can do with our lives is, *first*, to love You with all of our heart, soul, and mind. Second, You said to love our neighbor as ourselves (Matthew 22:37-39). *This* is my purpose—what You desire my entire life to be about. Yet You've given me a specific, personal way to live this out…You've given me a *mission*.

Thank You, God, that the way You've designed me is not a mistake. Every part of my gifts and personality work together to fulfill Your calling. Unveil a clear vision in my heart for the mission You've given me. Brush aside all other options and set my eyes on the path that You've specifically laid out for me.

In Jesus' name I pray.

—*Paige*

Finding Freedom in the Lord

*It is for freedom that Christ has set us free.
Stand firm, then, and do not let yourselves
be burdened again by a yoke of slavery.*

GALATIANS 5:1

Dear Lord, help me to separate myself from anything that keeps me from becoming all You made me to be. Liberate me from all habits of thought or feeling that are not Your best for my life. Teach me how to break free of everything that tries to control me other than You. Protect me from all plans of the enemy for my destruction so Your plan for my life will be fulfilled.

Lord, reveal any place in me where I am locked up. Help me to get free of whatever is in my life that is less than what You have for me. Thank You that even if I fail and go back to the thing from which You have set me free, You will still deliver me again (2 Corinthians 1:10). Liberate me from whatever could keep me from moving into all You have for me. Thank You that You are more powerful than anything I face.

In Jesus' name I pray.

—*Stormie*

97

I Feel Alone

I am with you and will watch over you
wherever you go…I will not leave you until I
have done what I have promised you.

GENESIS 28:15

Heavenly Father, my heart is hurting from the emptiness of feeling alone. At times, I feel invisible to others. Lord, I know You've given me a life that is precious, and I don't want to waste my time being focused on me. Fill my lonely emptiness with Your presence so that I won't shrink back as others pass by. Give me a heart that reaches out to others, just as You reach out to me when I overlook You.

Thank You for being with me and protecting me wherever I go. I choose to follow You because I know wherever You'll take me is exactly where I need to be. You will not steer me away from the good desires in my heart, but rather set me on the path to their fulfillment. You have shown me that Your plans for my life *far* exceed my own. The ultimate Father and Friend, You are everything I need. You've already promised You'd never leave my side…Lord, may I never leave *Yours*.

In Jesus' name I pray.

—*Paige*

Living a Holy Life

*Let us purify ourselves from everything that contaminates
body and spirit, perfecting holiness out of reverence for God.*

2 Corinthians 7:1

Dear Lord, I worship You in the beauty of Your holiness (Psalm 29:2). Only You are holy (1 Samuel 2:2). Yet You have called those who believe in You to be holy like You (Leviticus 19:2). I realize that the only way I can be holy is by following the leading of Your Holy Spirit in me. And I welcome You to help me get rid of anything in my life that is less than holy. Show me how to pursue holiness like You have said in Your Word to do (Hebrews 12:14).

Holy Spirit, crowd out anything in me that is not holy so that the beauty of Your holiness would beautify me in every possible way (2 Chronicles 20:21). You are the well from which I draw my own holiness, so help me to spend time with You every day for the fresh flow of Your Spirit in me that enables me to live a holy life.

In Jesus' name I pray.

—*Stormie*

Facing Troubles and Hard Times

Therefore we do not lose heart…For our light and momentary troubles are achieving for us an eternal glory that far outweighs them all.

2 Corinthians 4:16-17

Lord, I run to You for shelter in the midst of these hard times. I know that Your Word says not to be surprised when I suffer trials as though something strange and unexpected were happening (1 Peter 4:12). You told us that there would be troubles on this earth, but to take heart because You have overcome the world (John 16:33). You promise not only to comfort and carry us in the midst of our pain but to refine and complete us if we let You (James 1:3-4).

Lord, You call my trials *light* and *momentary*… which means You know something that I don't. You know the good that You will bring about and that my pain will only last for a moment in the grand scheme of things. Most of all, You know there *is* hope. Help me to see my circumstances from Your perspective and don't let me lose heart. The world may fall around me, but I am safe in the shade of Your hand.

In Jesus' name I pray.

—*Paige*

100

Seeking True Success

*For those God foreknew he also predestined
to be conformed to the image of his Son.*

ROMANS 8:29

Dear Lord, I know that true success is not about being rich, famous, or accomplished. It's about becoming all You created me to be and doing what You have called me to do and never violating that. Help me to walk close to You at all times so that I understand Your ways and Your heart toward me. Help me to trust that even when I go through times when I feel like I am anything but a success, that You are using that experience to help me become more like You.

Teach me not to judge the success of my life by what I see happening in the lives of others. I trust that You have called me and are preparing me to live the life of *true* success You have for me in Your perfect timing. I pray that everything You give me to do You will enable me to do well. I know that true success is fulfilling my purpose and glorifying You in all that I do.

In Jesus' name I pray.

—*Stormie*

Lord, I Long to Be Close to You

You, God, are my God, earnestly I seek you; I thirst for you, my whole being longs for you, in a dry and parched land where there is no water.

PSALM 63:1

Lord Jesus, I draw near to Your Presence. Only You can fill the void in my heart, for it was created for You. I long to know You and to hear Your voice. You are so precious to reveal Yourself to us and to actually desire a close relationship with Your children. Your Word says that through Your Spirit, we have the mind of Christ (1 Corinthians 2:16). Father, align my thoughts with Yours that I would begin to better understand Your ways. Lead me to think as You do and respond to situations with Your character.

Would You allow me into the very chambers of Your heart? It is there that I will find the most beautiful treasures that exist. Lord, You truly are my best friend. Yet I stand completely in humble awe before You. What a God of great measure. Father, let my lips be ever adorned with prayer and worship. May I be a woman who chases after Your own heart.

In Jesus' name I pray.

—Paige

102

When I Feel Powerless

*He gives strength to the weary and
increases the power of the weak.*

Isaiah 40:29

Lord, sometimes I feel powerless with regard to the things I want to see happen in my life. I am frustrated when I seem to have no control over my situation. But I know that it is not by my abilities but by *Your* power that good things happen. I don't have the power to change my life or my circumstances, but *You* do. It is the power of Your Spirit working in and through me that can transform my life.

I often feel pressured by outside circumstances, and sometimes I feel like I am stuck in one place and can't seem to move beyond it. So I ask that by the power of Your Spirit in me You would bring breakthrough in my life. I know when I walk with You I am never standing still. Thank You that even when I can't see it, You are always working in my life. I am grateful to You for doing more in me than I can even imagine.

In Jesus' name I pray.

—*Stormie*

Save Me from My Pity Parties

*When I consider your heavens…the moon and the stars,
which you have set in place, what is mankind that you are
mindful of them, human beings that you care for them?*

PSALM 8:3-4

Father, I'm ashamed to admit how I've been acting lately. I've been grumbling around, throwing a childish fit over what "isn't fair" in my life. I've jealously compared myself to others and sulked over what I thought they have that I don't. The problem with this mindset is that every thought has the word *me* in it. What about *You*? What about *others*? Lord, forgive me. If I took the focus off of myself for a second, I would see how blessed I really am.

Help me to worship You the next time I am overwhelmed with feeling sorry for myself. I choose to dwell on Your goodness and the bigger picture of life. Father, open my eyes to the immense needs around me, that my own difficulties would be put into proper perspective. I refuse to take for granted the precious gifts You've given me. Who am I that You should even care for me? Yet You sent Your Son to die…*in my place.*

In Jesus' name I pray.

—*Paige*

104

How Can I Make a Difference?

*The eyes of the LORD run to and fro throughout
the whole earth, to show Himself strong on
behalf of those whose heart is loyal to Him.*

2 CHRONICLES 16:9 NKJV

Lord, I want to make a difference in the world. Equip me to accomplish something great for Your Kingdom that will help people come to know You and have a better life. I know I can't make that happen on my own, so I ask You to make me ready to do what You have called me to do. Enable me to rise above my own limitations and learn to depend on the power of Your Spirit to accomplish all that You have for me to do.

Thank You that You will not stop working in me until my heart is fully Yours and I am inspired, ignited, and led by Your Holy Spirit in all I do. I don't want to be like the people in Your Word who limited what You wanted to do through them because they did not remember Your power (Psalm 78:41-42). I want to live every day by the power of Your Spirit.

In Jesus' name I pray.

—*Stormie*

105

Feeling Out of Place

*Before I formed you in the womb I knew
you, before you were born I set you apart.*

JEREMIAH 1:5

Father, sometimes I feel like I don't belong. Throughout different times in my life I've felt unwanted, awkward, or just out of place. I pray that You'd heal my heart and help me not to dwell on those times or feel that way any longer. You have shown me through Your love, grace, and forgiveness that the place where I belong is with You. Scripture talks about how Christians are strangers and aliens here on earth, because our true home is in Your Kingdom yet to come. Our soul longs for where You've created us to be.

You *set me apart* before I was even born for a specific purpose, and have called me to be separate from the things of this world. Yet You have placed me here with a mission to be a light that reaches deep into the desperate darkness. Show me the place that You have given me here on earth and how to spend my time. I follow You, Lord, because You are my home. Wherever You are is where I belong.

In Jesus' name I pray.

—Paige

106

When I Want to Give Up

But if we hope for what we do not see, we
wait eagerly for it with perseverance.

ROMANS 8:25 NKJV

Lord, I have been hoping and praying for things
that I still do not see happening in my life and I ask
that You would give me the strength to persevere. Your
Word says that "tribulation produces perseverance"
(Romans 5:3). So help me to persevere by standing
strong when hard things happen.

Your Word also says that *self-control* leads to *perseverance* which leads to *godliness* (2 Peter 1:6). Help me
to be strong in my faith and take control of my fear that
the things I hope for will never happen. And if what I
am hoping for right now is out of Your will for my life,
show me how to line up my will with Yours. I want to
live in godliness and not the corruption that is in the
world. Holy Spirit, lead me away from any desire to
give up. Help me walk with You, be solid in Your Word,
and be determined to never stop praying.

In Jesus' name I pray.

—*Stormie*

Waiting on My Future

Be still, and know that I am God.

PSALM 46:10

Father, You know all of the dreams that are stored up in my heart. Help me to be patient and wait on Your timing for their fulfillment. Thank You for the way You're weaving every detail in my life together and bringing deep desires You've placed in me to fruition. Help me not to grow restless where I am, for I know every moment is part of Your divine plan.

You are God over my past, present, and future, and You've been writing my life's story all along. I take comfort in knowing that Your Word says You will fight for me…I only need to be still (Exodus 14:14). Father, I rest in You, trusting that You will fight for my dreams, my hope, and my future. In my stillness, I look to You to show me how I can prepare for the things You're going to bring about in my life. I know this is not a time to sit back and do nothing, but rather *in faith* to prepare for what's ahead! Open my eyes to what You are doing in my life at this very moment.

In Jesus' name I pray.

—*Paige*

I Have Unfulfilled Dreams

He fulfills the desires of those who fear him;
he hears their cry and saves them.

PSALM 145:19

Dear Lord, I am so thankful that You care about the dreams I have in my heart because You have put some of them there. I have dreams in my heart that I long to see fulfilled, but I surrender them to You because I want my dreams to line up with Your plans for my life. I don't want to follow a dream of my own making that You will not bless because it is outside of Your will. I want to follow You and see the fulfillment of the dreams that *You* put in my heart.

If there is any dream in my heart that is not Your will for my life, help me to see and understand that. Show me clearly what it is and give me assurance and peace about it as You replace it with one that is far better. I need to know that the dreams in my heart are from You and that You will bless and fulfill them in Your way and Your time.

In Jesus' name I pray.

—*Stormie*

Finding Your Strength in My Weakness

My grace is sufficient for you, for my power is made perfect in weakness.

2 CORINTHIANS 12:9

Lord Jesus, I come before You surrendering my weaknesses. I lay down my physical, emotional, and even aptitude deficiencies. I praise You for being bigger than all of them! God, You have fashioned me from the inside out exactly how You want me to be. You have given me my gifts and abilities, and You also have allowed my weaknesses. Though at times out of pride I would rather hide and bury them all, You have revealed that they are *key* in displaying Your power.

In physical pain, You are my strength. In emotional battles, You are my victory. And Lord, in the abilities where I'm weak, You are my power! I will not be ashamed of my weaknesses, because You've declared them the way that You work most powerfully through me! Thank You, Father, that I can *boast* in my difficulties, because they bring about the most beautiful opportunities to experience You. For when I am weak, then I am strong (2 Corinthians 12:10).

In Jesus' name I pray.

—*Paige*

Seeing God's Light in Dark Times

When Jesus spoke again to the people, he said, "I am the light of the world. Whoever follows me will never walk in darkness, but will have the light of life."

JOHN 8:12

Dear Lord, I am grateful that You are the light of the world and the light of my life. No matter what plan of darkness encroaches on me, Your light in me never dims. Regardless of what dark things happen in my life, Your light in me always shines brightly, illuminating my life. You are the true Light which gives light to everyone who seeks You (John 1:9). Thank You that You are light and in You there is no darkness at all (1 John 1:5).

Help me to not be attracted to, or lured by, the many other lights in the world, for they all fail. Your light is constant because You are constant and never change. When I enter what seems to be a dark time in my life, help me to remember that I have Your light in me and Your light can never be put out.

In Jesus' name I pray.

—*Stormie*

111

When I Feel Shame

*Those who look to him are radiant; their
faces are never covered with shame.*

PSALM 34:5

Heavenly Father, there is a sick guilt that's settled over my soul. I feel stained by the wrong that I've done and I know only You can wipe that away. Lord, I don't hold back, but I confess to You *everything* that I know I've done against You. Forgive me also for hidden sins that I'm unaware of (Psalm 19:12). Through Your strength, I walk in a new direction and I won't ever look back.

Thank You that Your Word clearly says there is *no condemnation* for those who are in Christ Jesus (Romans 8:1). Though Satan tries to accuse me day and night before you (Revelation 12:10), You have washed my sins away and by Your blood I stand blameless in Your sight. When You died for my sins You also died for my shame. You have set my heart free and bestowed a crown of beauty on my head instead of ashes (Isaiah 61:3). I can't imagine why You would do this for me, but Lord…*I am so grateful!* I stand as a new woman by Your mercy and grace.

In Jesus' name I pray.

—*Paige*

I Want to Be a Whole Person

*A merry heart makes a cheerful countenance, but
by sorrow of the heart the spirit is broken.*

PROVERBS 15:13 NKJV

Lord, I ask You to restore all that is broken in me. I know that life doesn't work when any part of me is broken, so I pray that the only brokenness in me is where You are breaking down any resistance I have to doing things Your way. Where my spirit is broken because of sin in my life, I confess it to You and ask You to forgive me and restore me to a right relationship with You. Help me to forgive myself if not living Your way has broken my spirit.

Where someone else has been abusive in my life and broken my spirit, help me to forgive them. Mend my heart and restore me completely as only You can do. Touch me with Your healing power and cause my will not to hurt anymore. Restore my inner self to the wholeness You created me to enjoy in Your presence. Bring the wholeness I need to fully become the person You have made me to be.

In Jesus' name I pray.

—*Stormie*

I Am Cherished

*Since you are precious and honored in my sight, and because
I love you, I will…nations in exchange for your life.*

ISAIAH 43:4

Heavenly Father, Your love is the strongest that I've ever experienced. It's the most pursuing, yet patient love I have ever felt. I can't believe that Your Word says You've numbered the hairs on my head (Matthew 10:30). You care about every little detail about me. Scripture says Your love is so great that I need Your power to even grasp how wide, long, high, and deep it is (Ephesians 3:17-18). Your love fills out a dimension that my mind can't even fathom.

Scripture says You have chosen me to be Your treasured possession (Deuteronomy 7:6). This leaves me speechless. I stand in awe of the awesome Creator, Father, Savior, Lord, and Friend that You are. Thank You for loving me and cherishing me as Your Word and Life proves that You do. You have set a seal of ownership on me and placed a deposit in my heart, Your Holy Spirit, guaranteeing that I am Yours (2 Corinthians 1:22). I love, because *You first loved me* (1 John 4:19).

In Jesus' name I pray.

—Paige

How Do I Honor My Parents?

"Honor your father and mother"—which is the first commandment with a promise—"so that it may go well with you and that you may enjoy long life on the earth."

Ephesians 6:2-3

Dear Lord, I pray that You will help me to honor my father and mother. Whether they are alive or dead, whether they are with me or not, I know it is your command to give them honor. Teach me to recognize their good qualities and to forget their mistakes. Where I have been mistreated or abandoned in any way by them, help me to forgive them. Enable me not to hold against them the ways in which they are imperfect.

I don't want to shorten my life and bring misery upon myself because I have rebelled against Your only commandment that carries with it a promise of a long and good life. Help me to honor my parents by speaking *about* them and *to* them with great respect. I confess as sin any time I have not done that and I ask You to forgive me. Cleanse my heart of everything that is unloving and disrespectful.

In Jesus' name I pray.

—Stormie

I Feel So Restless

*He who began a good work in you will carry it
on to completion until the day of Christ Jesus.*

PHILIPPIANS 1:6

Lord, I'm struggling with where I am right now. I feel perpetually stuck and stranded, longing for where I'd really like to be and what I'd love to be doing. If there is anything holding me back that I've done or allowed, please remove it completely. If there's a step You've asked me to take that I haven't, please show me and help me move forward. However, if I'm exactly where You want me to be, give me a clear peace about it and contentment while I wait.

Open my eyes to the current blessings that I have around me. You've said it's Your will for me to be joyful and give thanks in all circumstances (1 Thessalonians 5:16-18), so I ask that You'd forgive me if I've had a complaining spirit lately. Thank You, Lord, that You're not about to leave me where I am, but You have plans to prosper me and to give me hope and a future (Jeremiah 29:11). My heart is thrilled to know that Your plans for me far exceed my own.

In Jesus' name I pray.

—*Paige*

Will God Provide for Me?

*My God will meet all your needs according
to the riches of his glory in Christ Jesus.*

PHILIPPIANS 4:19

Lord, I praise You and thank You that You are my provider and You never forsake Your people or fail to provide for those who look to You. I ask You to bless the finances I have, or will have. Help me to always have good work and enable me to find favor with the people I work for. I pray that You will teach me to gain finances according to Your will, for Your Word says that Your financial blessings do not bring sorrow (Proverbs 10:22).

Give me wisdom to handle money wisely and not do anything foolish. Help me to give to You and to others as You require, because I know I will never lack when I do (Proverbs 28:27). I pray that there will be no financial disasters in my future. You have said to seek You first and the things we need will be provided for us (Luke 12:29-31). I seek You for everything and I am thankful that "those who seek You shall not lack any good thing" (Psalm 34:10 NKJV).

In Jesus' name I pray.

—*Stormie*

Lord, Test My Heart

*Search me, God, and know my heart; test
me and know my anxious thoughts.*

Psalm 139:23

Lord, You know me. You know the words in my mouth before I even say them (Psalm 139:4). I come before You raw and exposed, laying myself down before Your throne. Often I try to hide my flaws and failures, foolishly thinking that I can somehow distract You from seeing they're there. But Jesus, You've engraved me on the palms of Your hands (Isaiah 49:16). I am ever before You.

Father, I don't want anything in me that shouldn't be there. I want to be pure before You. Test my heart and see if there is any offensive way in me, and lead me in the way everlasting (Psalm 139:24). Your Word says You search our hearts and examine our minds and reward us according to what You find (Jeremiah 17:10). Teach me Your way so I will walk in truth, and give me an undivided heart that I may fear Your name (Psalm 86:11). Thank You, Lord, for cleansing me from head to toe. May my heart be blameless in Your sight.

In Jesus' name I pray.

—*Paige*

118

Finding Favor with God and Others

Let love and faithfulness never leave you; bind them around your neck, write them on the tablet of your heart. Then you will win favor and a good name in the sight of God and man.

PROVERBS 3:3-4

Lord, I want to find favor in Your sight and in the sight of others as well. Enable me to do what is right and to live my life with Your mercy and truth in my heart. Help me never to forget what You teach me, so that it becomes visible on the outside as well as deep within me. Finding favor with You is more important to me than anything else.

Whenever I am with anyone, I pray that they will see the beauty of Your Spirit in me, even if they cannot yet identify what it is. May Your love in my heart not only affect the way I act at all times, but also the way I think and speak to people. I pray that when I am with others, Your presence in me will become real and apparent to them.

In Jesus' name I pray.

—Stormie

Preserve My Reputation

*A good name is more desirable than great riches;
to be esteemed is better than silver or gold.*

PROVERBS 22:1

Lord, I'm feeling attacked as others are trying to bring me down. I know Your Word says that we should expect to be persecuted when we follow in Your steps (1 Peter 2:21). Even still, You said that we should live such good lives among unbelievers that, though they try to accuse us, they are ashamed because they cannot find any fault (Titus 2:8). Lord, people tease me because of my high standards and desire to please You. They try to get me to slip up and go against Your will for me. Keep me strong and bold, but gracious and able to withstand the devil's tactics. I am Your daughter, set apart for a higher purpose, and I *will not* betray You. Protect my reputation, Lord.

Give me integrity, that my daily life might be pure and upright. Preserve the good name You've given me that I might be a worthy ambassador for You. In Jesus' name I proclaim that there is no slander, no lies, no scheme that can come against me, because I am covered by Your precious blood.

In Jesus' name I pray.

—*Paige*

Welcoming God's Presence

*If your Presence does not go with us, do
not send us up from here.*

EXODUS 33:15

Dear Lord, I welcome Your presence in my life. I long to always live in Your presence, because I know it is the only true place of safety and blessing. Just like Moses said, I don't want to be where Your presence is not. I know You are everywhere but the fullness and power of Your presence is only found with those who have a passion to know and love You. Help me to maintain that passion at all times.

Thank You, Jesus, that You are Immanuel—God who is with us. Because of Your Holy Spirit in me, I am never alone. I have Your presence within me always, and whenever I turn to You in prayer, in worship, or in Your Word, I can hear You speak to my heart. Keep me from anything or anyone who denies, rejects, minimizes, or disregards Your existence. Enable me to separate myself from whoever or whatever tries to undermine Your powerful presence in my life.

In Jesus' name I pray.

—*Stormie*

Consume Me with Your Fire

Therefore, since we are receiving a kingdom that cannot be shaken, let us...so worship God acceptably with reverence and awe, for our "God is a consuming fire."

Hebrews 12:28-29

Lord Jesus, light a fire in my soul that cannot be quenched. Let Your Spirit in me burn away everything that is not of You until only You remain. Scripture says that Your children shine like the stars in the universe as we hold out the Word of Life (Philippians 2:15-16). You reveal evidence of Yourself through us so that a dark and dying world might see our light and run to it. You've lit this spark in me so that it might catch on and ignite everyone and everything I touch.

The only way that I won't burn out is by continually surrendering myself to You, depending on the fire of Your Holy Spirit to sustain me. You are the anchor for my soul—holding me firm and secure (Hebrews 6:19). I am unwavering because I know my hope and future cannot be shaken. Lord, consume me with Your fire.

In Jesus' name I pray.

—*Paige*

122

Saving Good Relationships

*Two are better than one, because they have a
good return for their labor: If either of them
falls down, one can help the other up.*

ECCLESIASTES 4:9-10

Lord, help me to value my relationships with good friends, for I know that godly friends contribute to each other's lives. Teach me to be a friend who is encouraging and uplifting. Help me to never be critical, judgmental, or opinionated with others, but to always speak the truth in love. Help my friends and me to never speak badly of one another to anyone.

Enable me to be slow to respond in any selfish way and quick to forgive. When my friend does or says something that upsets me, keep me from throwing away a good relationship just because there are mistakes or misunderstandings. Be in charge of all my relationships so that the enemy cannot come between us to cause friction or separation. Help me to recognize the relationships that are worth the time and effort it takes to keep them strong. Teach me to be a friend who "loves at all times" (Proverbs 17:17).

In Jesus' name I pray.

—*Stormie*

123

Starving for Redemption

Do not fear, for I have redeemed you; I have summoned you by name; you are mine.

ISAIAH 43:1

Lord Jesus, thank You that no matter what I've done, the Power of Your forgiveness is always strong enough to wipe it away. Your Word says, "Everyone who calls on the name of the Lord will be saved" (Romans 10:13), so I cry out to You and declare my faith in Your name. Though we have all fallen short of Your glory, we are justified freely through the redemption that You gave us through Jesus Christ (Romans 3:23-24).

Thank You that *while I was still a sinner*, You died for me (Romans 5:8). You've traded in my filthy rags and clothed me with Your beautiful robes of righteousness. Your unfailing love is as high as the heavens and Your faithfulness reaches to the clouds (Psalm 57:10). Father, You have been pursuing me and fighting for my heart in ways that I can't even fathom. You hold the victory of this battle as You've delivered me from the hand of the enemy. You have redeemed me and I am Yours.

In Jesus' name I pray.

—*Paige*

When Everything
Is Going Right

Continue in what you have learned and
have become convinced of, because you know
those from whom you learned it.

2 TIMOTHY 3:14

Dear Lord, over and over in Your Word there are stories of people who turned to You in times of trouble and You saved them and brought them to a good place. Yet when things were going well they forgot You and didn't turn to You until the next disaster came along. Help me not to be like that. When everything is going well in my life, help me to be especially careful to be in Your Word and to pray just as much if not more.

Your Word says, "Let him who thinks he stands take heed lest he fall" (1 Corinthians 10:12 NKJV). I don't want to think that just because I am standing strong one day that I am invincible and won't fall. Help me to never forget for a moment how I must always depend on You. Enable me to seek You in the time of blessing as well as in times of need.

In Jesus' name I pray.

—*Stormie*

Lord, Help Me Be Real

*I know, my God, that you test the heart
and are pleased with integrity.*

1 CHRONICLES 29:17

Heavenly Father, remove the walls I've built around myself that shouldn't be there. Help me to be real and genuine that others may see Your light and work in me. Forgive me for putting up fronts and pretending to be something I'm not just to impress others. Take off and throw out each mask that I've hidden under, and give me the courage to show the raw and real woman You've created. You've forgiven me, You've redeemed me, and You've approved me…what more do I need?

Scripture says whoever walks with integrity walks securely (Proverbs 10:9). Father, I know that having integrity means *really being* who I say I am. Give me a pure and honest heart, that others would be refreshed by the genuine evidence of You in me. Help me to be real so that others might feel the freedom to come out from hiding and reveal their true selves. You've given me a story and You've been too good for me to keep it to myself. With Your hand I step out and dare to live free.

In Jesus' name I pray.

—*Paige*

Give Me a Right Heart

Create in me a pure heart, O God, and
renew a steadfast spirit within me.

Psalm 51:10

Dear Lord, I pray that You would purify my heart. Create in me a clean heart and renew a right spirit within me. Take away any thoughts, feelings, or obsessions from me that are not glorifying to You. I know that when my heart is pure and right it pleases You, and I want to please You more than anything. I also know that a pure heart is pleasant to others, because out of it come words and actions that are uplifting.

There is no way I can have a right heart without You making it clean (Proverbs 20:9). I ask You to fill me afresh with Your love so that it crowds out anything in me that is unloving. Show me the condition of my heart as I read Your Word, which reveals "the thoughts and intents of the heart" (Hebrews 4:12 NKJV). Help me to keep a close watch over my heart because I know it cannot be trusted (Proverbs 4:23).

In Jesus' name I pray.

—*Stormie*

Lord, Don't Let Me Be Lukewarm

Do not merely listen to the word, and so deceive yourselves. Do what it says.

JAMES 1:22

Lord, don't let my love for You be mild. Your heart must break as You love Your children with all You have, and too often watch it returned with stale, empty words. Jesus, You deserve *so much more*. You asked Your disciple Peter three times if he truly loved You with an unconditional, *agape* love…and he could only say he loved You with brotherly, *phileo* love. Yet again You told him, "Follow Me" (John 21:15-19).

Father, I refuse to slander Your name by saying I'm a Christian and not *actually* following You. Your Word says You'd rather us either be hot or cold with our faith, but if we are lukewarm, You'll spit us out of Your mouth (Revelation 3:15-16)! Set my heart ablaze with passionate and limitless love for You. Every day, may I fall more and more in love with my God. Forgive me for ever loving You less than You deserve. You said to choose this day whom I will serve (Joshua 24:15)…I choose You, with all of my heart.

In Jesus' name I pray.

—Paige

Making Hope a Habit

May the God of hope fill you with all joy and
peace as you trust in him, so that you may overflow
with hope by the power of the Holy Spirit.

ROMANS 15:13

Lord, I thank You that You are the God of hope and that because of Your Holy Spirit in me, I can be filled with Your hope at all times (Romans 5:5). Thank You that no matter what is happening to me or around me I always have a reason to put my hope in You. Let Your hope in me crowd out any hopelessness I may have about anything.

I commit to reading Your Word often because I know it was written for my comfort and hope (Romans 15:4). "I have put my hope in your word" (Psalm 119:81). Prepare me to "give a defense to everyone who asks… a reason for the hope that is in" me (1 Peter 3:15 NKJV). Give me such joy because of Your hope in me that it overflows to others who see it and are attracted to it enough to find out why (Psalm 146:5).

In Jesus' name I pray.

—*Stormie*

God, You Really Want to Use *Me*?

Here is my servant, whom I uphold, my chosen one in whom I delight; I will put my Spirit on him, and he will bring justice to the nations.

ISAIAH 42:1

Lord, is it true? You really want to use *me*? Speak to my heart, Father, and remind me of exactly why You've placed me here. It's so hard to imagine that after all the ways I've fallen short, You still haven't given up on me. Thank You that Your desire to use me has nothing to do with what I have to offer. Whatever gifts and abilities I have come from You. You're amazing.

I pray that for every door that has shut in my life, You would open two more. You are the Lord of my future, the Bearer of my hope. Your Spirit inside of me builds and equips me daily to do more than I could ever imagine. I give You the only thing that You actually *need* to use me: a willing and trusting heart. Thank You that when rejection slams in my face, Your words to me are…"Yes, I have chosen *you*."

In Jesus' name I pray.

—*Paige*

Prayer That Makes a Difference

The prayer of a righteous person is powerful and effective.

JAMES 5:16

Dear Lord, I want my prayers to make a positive difference in my life and in the lives of others. Your Word says that prayer is effective when a righteous person prays with great concern, energy, and heartfelt care. Lord Jesus, I know that You alone have made me righteous, and because You have sent Your Holy Spirit to live in me I am being perfected from the inside out. Help me not to do anything that would interfere with that process.

Because Your Word says that any sin in my life interferes with my prayers getting answered, I confess all my sin to You. Where I am not seeing it, reveal it to me. I don't want any sin in my heart to cause You to hold off answering my prayer until it is cleared up between us (Psalm 66:18). Teach me to pray with passion and guide me in every prayer so that I can pray with life-changing power.

In Jesus' name I pray.

—*Stormie*

Teach Me to Be Gracious

Let your conversation be always full of grace, seasoned with salt, so that you may know how to answer everyone.

COLOSSIANS 4:6

Father, I repent to You because I have had an attitude lately. I don't know why, but everything has been rubbing me the wrong way. Forgive me for grumbling under my breath and lashing out at others, especially You. You are *never* rough with me. Though You are firm, You are always so gentle and kind. I know I don't deserve Your beautiful compassion. How much more should I be gracious to those who could never offend me as much as I have offended You?

Lord, change my heart. Rid me of my negative thoughts, biting words, and poisonous attitudes. Fill me with Your thoughts that are pure, Your words that are lovely, and Your countenance that is admirable (Philippians 4:8). Help me to be gracious toward everyone I encounter. Give me extra grace for those I am closest to who tend to push my buttons. I long to be a blessing to them, especially. I give You my heart and ask that You transform it from bitterness into an overflowing well of Your gorgeous compassion.

In Jesus' name I pray.

—Paige

Staying Free of Destructive Relationships

Do not make friends with a hot-tempered person, do not associate with one easily angered, or you may learn their ways and get yourself ensnared.

PROVERBS 22:24-25

Lord, Your Word says that a good friend is not so changeable that You never know how they are going to act from day to day. Help me to never be like that, and to not continue in a relationship with someone who is like that. Enable me to recognize right away when a person is often angry, negative, and destructive toward me so that I won't continue on with them as a friend. Help me to be rid of any relationships in my life that are negative in an ongoing way.

Although I can't control how another person treats me, with Your help I can refuse to allow them to *continue* to treat me badly. Show me if I have any destructive relationship in my life and enable me to separate myself from that person. Help me to recognize that when a person continually makes me feel badly about myself and my life, they are not part of Your plan for me.

In Jesus' name I pray.

—*Stormie*

133

I Return to You

I have swept away your offenses like a cloud, your sins like the morning mist. Return to me, for I have redeemed you.

ISAIAH 44:22

Father, I don't know where I've been lately…but it hasn't been with You. I know You haven't left me; I'm the one who's walked away. Lord Jesus, I *return* to You. I declare that there is no one else and nothing for me on this earth besides You. Thank You that, unlike anyone else, I don't even have to explain myself to You, because *You know*. You welcome me back with open arms and I run to them.

Your Word says that nothing in all creation can separate me from Your love (Romans 8:39). I don't have to work my way to gain Your approval because I could never earn Your love; You freely gave it to me through Jesus Christ. I stand in awe of You and what You've done for me. Keep me close by Your side and chasing Your heart. After far too many days of wandering, I return to You, my home.

In Jesus' name I pray.

—*Paige*

Identifying My Enemy

Put on the full armor of God, so that you can take your stand against the devil's schemes. For our struggle is not against flesh and blood, but against the rulers, against the authorities, against the powers of this dark world and against the spiritual forces of evil in the heavenly realms.

EPHESIANS 6:11-12

Dear Lord, help me to always recognize that my real enemy is Your enemy, and Your enemy is mine. Teach me how to put on the "full armor of God" so that I can always successfully withstand the enemy's plans for my demise. Help me to take up the sword of the Spirit—which is Your Word—and the shield of faith in order to stop the darts of the wicked one. Make me strong and watchful in prayer because the enemy never rests.

Lord, help me to not see other people as my enemy. It's not the mean girl, or my boss, or a difficult family member, or any other person or group of people, but it is the *evil* one. Teach me to resist the devil with worship, Your Word, and prayer, knowing he will flee from me (James 4:7).

In Jesus' name I pray.

—*Stormie*

135

On the Edge of Rebellion

*Flee the evil desires of youth and pursue
righteousness, faith, love and peace, along with
those who call on the Lord out of a pure heart.*

2 TIMOTHY 2:22

Lord, I'm just going to be honest because You know my heart anyway. I feel like I'm on the brink of walking away from You and doing things that I know You wouldn't be pleased with. I feel restless and rebellious right now and I'm starting to desire things of this world more than You. *Forgive me.* Change my heart before I foolishly cross the line. Remind me of how beautiful and wonderful Your ways are and how nothing but pain awaits me anywhere else.

Draw me back to You and renew my perspective to see how Your promises and blessings are poured out on those who follow You. You've said that we will eat the fruit of our ways (Proverbs 1:31), and I fear where I'll end up if I don't turn my back on these rebellious desires and walk away. Your Word says no eye has seen and no ear has heard what You have prepared for those who love You (1 Corinthians 2:9). I choose You.

In Jesus' name I pray.

—*Paige*

136

Learning to Pray First

*But seek first his kingdom and his righteousness, and
all these things will be given to you as well.*

MATTHEW 6:33

Lord, You know the things I have need of before I even do, but You still want me to come before You and ask (Matthew 6:8). Help me remember to pray first, *before* I try to meet my own needs in my own way. Teach me to seek Your Kingdom in my life before I seek other things. Thank You that when I do that, You will give me all I need.

Help me to not worry about my life and my future. Teach me to remember that You have promised to respond to my prayers when I seek You before all else. I don't want to be so preoccupied with material things that I forget to turn to You every day and in all situations. When a need appears in my life, help me to turn to You in prayer before I let worry overtake me. Thank You that You will always supply everything I need when I ask it of You.

In Jesus' name I pray.

—*Stormie*

I'd Rather Be with You Than Anywhere

Whom have I in heaven but you? And earth has nothing I desire besides you.

PSALM 73:25

My dearest Jesus, it's such a joy to escape to You. Thank You for always being with me and lighting my way. I can find peace in any situation, perspective for every trial, and joy for any pain because of You. When I spend time with You all of my fears and worries melt away. It's only in Your presence that I feel truly safe, accepted, and whole. For once my heart feels fully alive and understood. You remind me of who I truly am… more importantly, Whose I am.

Lord, better is one day in Your courts than a thousand elsewhere (Psalm 84:10). I can come to You messy and empty and You fill me in the most lovely and delicate way. You know just how to speak to my heart and captivate my soul. This world has nothing for me—I desire You above all. You are precious to me, Lord. I love You with all of my heart.

In Jesus' name I pray.

—Paige

Not Letting Others Define Who I Am

*In your relationships with one another, have
the same mindset as Christ Jesus.*

PHILIPPIANS 2:5

Dear Lord, thank You that You accept me the way I am, but You are always growing and changing me to become more like You every day. I don't ever want my need for acceptance from others to cause me to make bad decisions. Help me to not let others define who I am or determine who I am to become. Only You know who You made me to be. Enable me to live true to who You say I am.

Help me to avoid the problems that arise when I try to live up to other people's standards for my life instead of Yours. As I seek You every day, fortify me with strength and a clear mind. Help me to reject anything any person has said about me that doesn't line up with what *You* say about me. Teach me to pray for others who clearly do not know Your ways and seek to undermine Your purpose for my life. Enable me to not let my weakness define who I am, but rather Your strength.

In Jesus' name I pray.

—*Stormie*

139

I Feel So Insecure

For God has not given us a spirit of fear, but of
power and of love and of a sound mind.

2 TIMOTHY 1:7 NKJV

Lord, my heart is weak. I'm so afraid someone will pull back the curtain and expose all that I've tried to hide. You know what I've been through that has brought me to this point…You know every moment of hurt and shame. I stand before You bare and vulnerable, but nothing surprises You because You know it already. When You look at me, You see Your beloved daughter. You see a bold and secure woman of God who is able to do anything You ask.

Your Word says that I am not of those who shrink back and are destroyed, but one who believes and is saved (Hebrews 10:39). Since, through You, I have died to the principles of this world, why do I still act as though I belong to it and submit to its rules (Colossians 2:20)? I claim Your Power over my life and ask that You would wash away any part of me that is still bound by the standards of this world. Remind me of who I am and what I'm worth.

In Jesus' name I pray.

—*Paige*

Praying with Other People

If two of you on earth agree about anything they ask for, it will be done for them by my Father in heaven.

MATTHEW 18:19

Lord Jesus, You have said that where two or three people are gathered together in Your name, You are there in the midst of them (Matthew 18:20). More than anything I desire Your presence in my life, especially when people pray together. You have said that if just two people agree in prayer, whatever we ask will be done by You, Lord. Help me to find one or more prayer partners with whom I can pray often. The promise of Your presence and the power of those prayers make the possibilities of doing so irresistible.

Give me the confidence that comes from knowing You and being led by Your Spirit to be able to suggest praying with someone else. There is so much to pray about and I don't want to hesitate to ask someone to pray with me because I am afraid. Give me the boldness to do this because I recognize that all things are possible when people pray together.

In Jesus' name I pray.

—*Stormie*

Lord, I'm Afraid

So do not fear, for I am with you; do not be dismayed,
for I am your God. I will strengthen you and help you;
I will uphold you with my righteous right hand.

ISAIAH 41:10

Father, there are certain fears that perpetually haunt me. Some are paralyzing, while others keep me continually distracted with stress. Lord, Your Word says over and over again, "Do not fear." I know this is not Your will for me. In Jesus' name, bind up the enemy who tries to take me captive and make me afraid of (specific fear). I know that Satan only has the power over me that I give him. Lord, You are stronger than anything I could ever be afraid of. With You on my side, whom shall I fear (Psalm 27:1)?

Jesus, when Your disciple Peter walked on water, he only started to sink when the wind kicked up and he began to fear. Father, don't let me give in to the fear which keeps me from walking out my destiny and causes me to sink into the sea of despair. When I go to sleep, calm my mind and fill me with thoughts that are lovely and full of the hope that You have for me. I depend on You.

In Jesus' name I pray.

—*Paige*

You're All That I Need

*His divine power has given us everything we need
for a godly life through our knowledge of him
who called us by his own glory and goodness.*

2 PETER 1:3

Dear Lord, I am forever grateful that You have not only given me life with You for eternity, but that You have given me everything I need in this life as well. Help me to remember this in the times when I doubt that You will provide for me. Teach me to cling to the truth that You have given me "exceedingly great and precious promises" (2 Peter 1:4) and through these I can become more like You and see the power of Your Spirit at work on my behalf.

Forgive me for any time I doubt that Your promises are for me. Increase my faith to believe You and not fear for my future. Help me to dwell on Your Word and not on my own needs. Enable me to trust completely that You are all I need. Because I have You, You will provide everything for me to live the good life of power and purpose You have for me.

In Jesus' name I pray.

—*Stormie*

143

Lord, Save My Loved One

*God our Savior…wants all people to be saved
and to come to a knowledge of the truth.*

1 TIMOTHY 2:3-4

Father, You are so good. Thank You that though we are a sinful and rebellious people, You still desire with *all Your heart* that we accept Your salvation. Jesus, I am burdened as I think of how (*name of person*) doesn't know You as his/her Lord and Savior. Scripture says that You don't want anyone to perish but everyone to come to repentance (2 Peter 3:9). I lift up those words to You and ask that You would spare my loved one. Forgive their rebellion and draw them to Yourself through the power of Your Holy Spirit.

I ask in Jesus' name that Your Presence would meet them right now and stir in their heart. Pursue them in such a way that they cannot ignore. Your Word says that Satan blinds the eyes of unbelievers so they cannot see the Truth of the Gospel (2 Corinthians 4:4). Lord, *unveil their eyes* and pierce the darkness with Your light. Demolish the stronghold that the enemy has over them and radically transform their life. I entrust them to Your loving hands.

In Jesus' name I pray.

—*Paige*

Embracing the Moment

For our light affliction, which is but for a moment,
is working for us a far more exceeding and eternal
weight of glory, while we do not look at the things
which are seen, but at the things which are not
seen. For the things which are seen are temporary,
but the things which are not seen are eternal.

2 CORINTHIANS 4:17-18 NKJV

Dear Lord, whenever I am tempted to become afraid or uncertain about the future, help me to remember that You are with me (Philippians 4:13). When I feel panicked about a situation that is happening in my life, or may *possibly* happen in my life, enable me to embrace the moment I am in by embracing You in it. Teach me to not look at what is seen and temporary, but rather to focus on the unseen things which are eternal.

Help me to remember—even when my life is especially hard—that You will provide everything I need for the moment I am in. When things don't happen the way I hoped or planned, open my eyes to the blessings that are right in front of me (Proverbs 20:13).

In Jesus' name I pray.

—*Stormie*

Drama with Friends

*If it is possible, as far as it depends on
you, live at peace with everyone.*

ROMANS 12:18

Father, I lift up my friendship with (*name of person*)
to You right now. I care about her/him deeply, but we've
been having some problems lately. I ask that You would
open my eyes to understand their position, what they are
going through, and what they need most at this moment.
Give me insight by Your Spirit as to how I can bless them.
Reveal any ways that I have wronged them and help me
to humbly ask for their forgiveness. Your Word says that
I must reconcile myself to them *first* before I enter into
Your Presence to worship (Matthew 5:23-24).

Lord, please remove any bitter seeds that have
grown up in me because of hurtful things my friend
has said or done. Scripture reminds me that I shouldn't
be so sensitive to people's words, for I know how many
times I have carelessly said unpleasant things about oth-
ers (Ecclesiastes 7:21-22). Help me not to be a person
who drops people when I'm offended and burns bridges
quickly. Allow me to love and embrace others, just as
You do for me.

In Jesus' name I pray.

—*Paige*

Praying for My Country

If my people who are called by my name will humble themselves, and pray…then I will hear from heaven, and forgive their sin and heal their land.

2 Chronicles 7:14

Lord, I pray that You will bless my nation. Raise up wise and godly leaders who have the welfare of the people as their priority and concern, and who do the right thing so that we can lead the kind of peaceful lives you have promised in Your Word (1 Timothy 2:1-2). There is so much in the world and in my country that makes me anxious and afraid, but You have said to pray about everything that concerns me instead of worrying, and if I do, Your peace will guard my heart and mind (Philippians 4:6-7). Show me how I should pray in specific ways.

I ask that You would pour out Your Spirit on every part of this country and especially on the town where I live. Expose evil and remove it from among us. Take corrupt leaders out of power. Protect us from the enemy's plans to harm us. Keep danger, disaster, and violence far from us.

In Jesus' name I pray.

—*Stormie*

Lord, Send Me a Mentor

As iron sharpens iron, so one person sharpens another.

PROVERBS 27:17

Lord, there is so much going on in my life that I desire to share with someone who's older and wiser than me. Your Word is the foundation for my life, yet my heart craves fellowship with a godly woman who has already walked the path that I'm on. I would love someone to sit with who would share her story with me in order to bring perspective to my own.

Scripture is always saying that a wise person accepts instruction and seeks noble advice (Proverbs 19:20). Your Word also confirms that our plans fail if we lack counsel, but with many advisers they will succeed (Proverbs 15:22). Father, would You bring a godly mentor into my life? Would You connect me with a woman who is willing to invest in me, challenge me, and believe in me? Most of all, I ask for a mentor whose heart is directly in line with Yours. I pray that I could be just as much a blessing to her as she is to me. Thank You in advance for Your handpicked provision.

In Jesus' name I pray.

—*Paige*

Getting Free of Addictions

All things are lawful for me, but all things are not helpful. All things are lawful for me, but I will not be brought under the power of any.

1 Corinthians 6:12 nkjv

Lord, where there is something in my life that has the potential to become an addiction, I pray You would enable me to be free of it. Help me to never play around with anything that has the potential to harm me. I don't want to follow the crowd or the voice of the enemy, nor do I want to take any kind of harmful substance to make myself feel better instead of relying on You to fulfill my life. I know that taking something to alter my mood can lure me into a trap of delusion that will keep me from all You have for me.

Take away any tendency in me to have an addictive personality, including any unhealthy relationship or eating disorder. I don't want food to fill an emptiness in me that can only be filled with more of You. Help me to resist even things that may not be bad in and of themselves but are not good for me personally.

In Jesus' name I pray.

—*Stormie*

Prayer for a Suicidal Friend

*He will wipe every tear from their eyes. There will
be no more death or mourning or crying or pain,
for the old order of things has passed away.*

REVELATION 21:6

Lord, I submit my friend (*name of friend*) to You right now. My heart is desperately burdened and troubled on their behalf. The enemy is heavily upon them, gripping them with depression and the temptation of suicide. In Jesus' name, I ask that You would deliver my friend from Satan's scheme to destroy them. Send Your angels to fight for and protect them in this battle for their very soul and life. Your Word says that everyone who lives has hope (Ecclesiastes 9:4)! I proclaim life, hope, and a future over my friend right now.

You are close to the brokenhearted and save those who are crushed in spirit (Psalm 34:18). Jesus, You have died and overcome the grave so that we can *live!* You have given all who believe a hope that cannot be cut off (Proverbs 23:18): a beautiful relationship with You on earth and an eternity in heaven with the Father. Breathe this very life and hope into my friend at this moment. Holy Spirit, *rescue* them!

In Jesus' name I pray.

—*Paige*

150

Help Me Understand the Bible

Your word is a lamp for my feet, a light on my path.

PSALM 119:105

Lord, I know that Your Word is food for my soul and I need it like I need food for my body. But sometimes the Bible is hard to understand. Help me to read it every day and truly comprehend what You are desiring to teach me. My heart is open to all You have to show me and I don't want to miss anything that I should know. Make the words come alive to me with their true meaning.

I don't want to just read Your Word; I want to do what it says. But I know I can't do it perfectly without Your help. Enable me to respond to it with an obedient heart. Thank You that Your Word is "living and powerful…and is a discerner of the thoughts and intents of the heart" (Hebrews 4:12). Show me in Your Word how to be who You made me to be. Thank You that anyone who trusts in You and obeys Your Word will find a good and happy life (Proverbs 16:20). I want that for my future.

In Jesus' name I pray.

—*Stormie*

151

Restoration with Parents

You who are younger, submit yourselves to your elders. All of you, clothe yourselves with humility toward one another.

1 Peter 5:5

Heavenly Father, I bring before Your throne my relationship with my mother and father. You know every detail of my life—all of the ways that they have wronged me and I have wronged them. I release my pain and anger to You, asking for Your Spirit to give me the strength to forgive. Scripture says that it's to my glory to overlook an offense (Proverbs 19:11), so I turn my eyes upon *You* instead of how I've been hurt. Give me a heart to treat both of my parents with overwhelming compassion and help me to honor them as I know Your Word says that is the first commandment with a promise (Ephesians 6:1-3).

Lord, I ask that You would bind up any wounds that my mother or father has and restore them to Yourself in every way. Please speak to their soul about the issues between us that need to be resolved. Soften and convict each of us so that we can come together and be beautifully reconciled. Father, hear the cry of my heart.

In Jesus' name I pray.

—*Paige*

Worshipping God *His* Way

*Although they knew God, they did not glorify Him
as God, nor were thankful, but became futile in their
thoughts, and their foolish hearts were darkened.*

ROMANS 1:21 NKJV

Lord, there are countless reasons to praise You and I don't want to neglect any of them. I want to worship You for *all* that You are. I praise You because You are my Heavenly Father and You love me unconditionally. I worship You as the Creator and Lord of all. There is no other God but You. I worship You as the God of love, joy, peace, mercy, and truth. I praise You because Your Word is unfailing and You are the same today as You were yesterday and will be tomorrow. I thank You that You and Your Word are unchanging and I can always depend on that.

Thank You for sending Your Son, Jesus, to die for me so I can be forgiven and spend eternity with You. Thank You that You, Jesus, are my healer, deliverer, and provider. Thank You for sending Your Holy Spirit to dwell in me and be my comforter and guide. Thank You that You will never leave or forsake me.

In Jesus' name I pray.

—Stormie

153

I Want to Be a Light

*You are the light of the world…let your light
shine before others, that they may see your good
deeds and glorify your Father in heaven.*

MATTHEW 5:14-16

Lord, You have placed Your light in me to shine in this dark world. You have not called me to hide my light from others—Your Word says no one would light a lamp and put it under a bowl (Matthew 5:15). Rather, You have given me this light that I might let it *shine* and take it into the darkest of places.

Scripture says that You are the light of the world and whoever follows You will never walk in darkness, but will have the light of life (John 8:12). Thank You that because I am Yours, I will never be overtaken by darkness. I can boldly walk in the midst of it, but I will never be overshadowed. The light inside of me is Your Presence itself, and nothing can stand against its power. Illuminate Your salvation, love, and truth through me, that the world would be blinded to all else…and only see *You*.

In Jesus' name I pray.

—*Paige*

154

Transforming My Life

The Lord is the Spirit; and where the Spirit
of the Lord is, there is freedom.

2 Corinthians 3:17

Lord, I am so very grateful that You are constant and unchanging. Thank You that Your Spirit in me is constant and unchanging too. Thank You that where Your Spirit is, there is liberty. Whenever I look to You, I am being transformed by Your Spirit into Your image— from glory to glory (2 Corinthians 3:18). Help me to always reflect Your beauty. Keep me from looking at anything that would take away from Your glory in me.

Help me to value Your presence in my life more than I value anything else. I don't ever want to do anything to hinder the transforming work You want to do in me. When I look in the mirror I want to see You reflected back. When other people look at me I want them to see Your radiance too. Thank You that You have the power to set me free from anything in my life that would keep me from all You have for me.

In Jesus' name I pray.

—*Stormie*